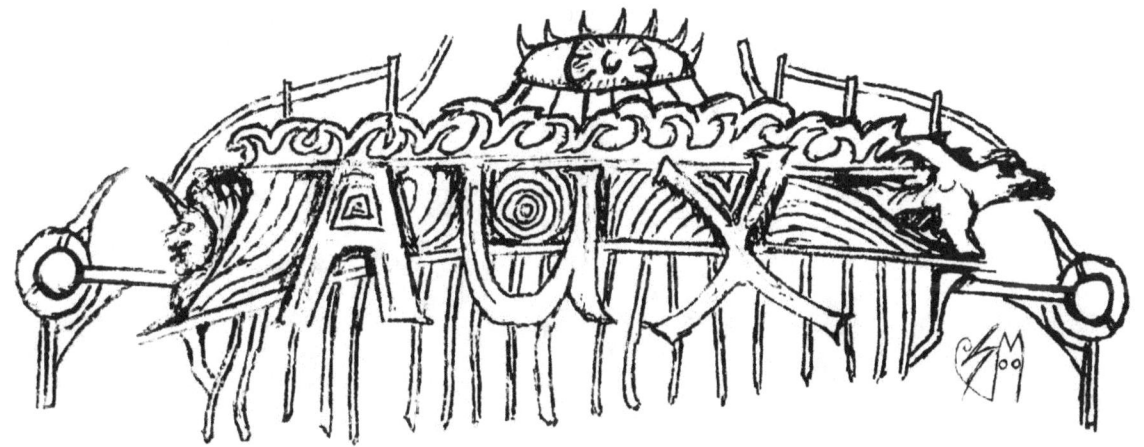

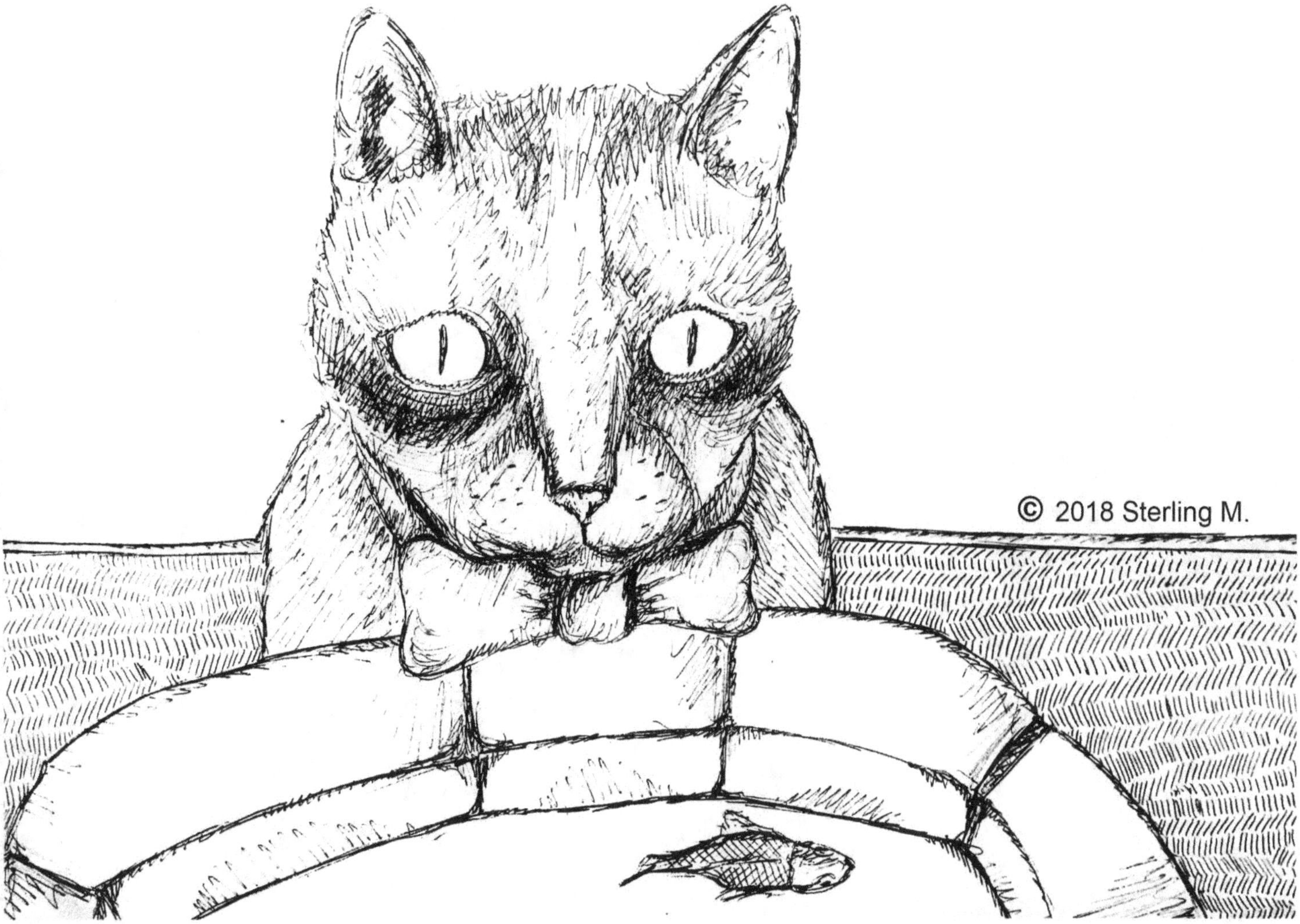

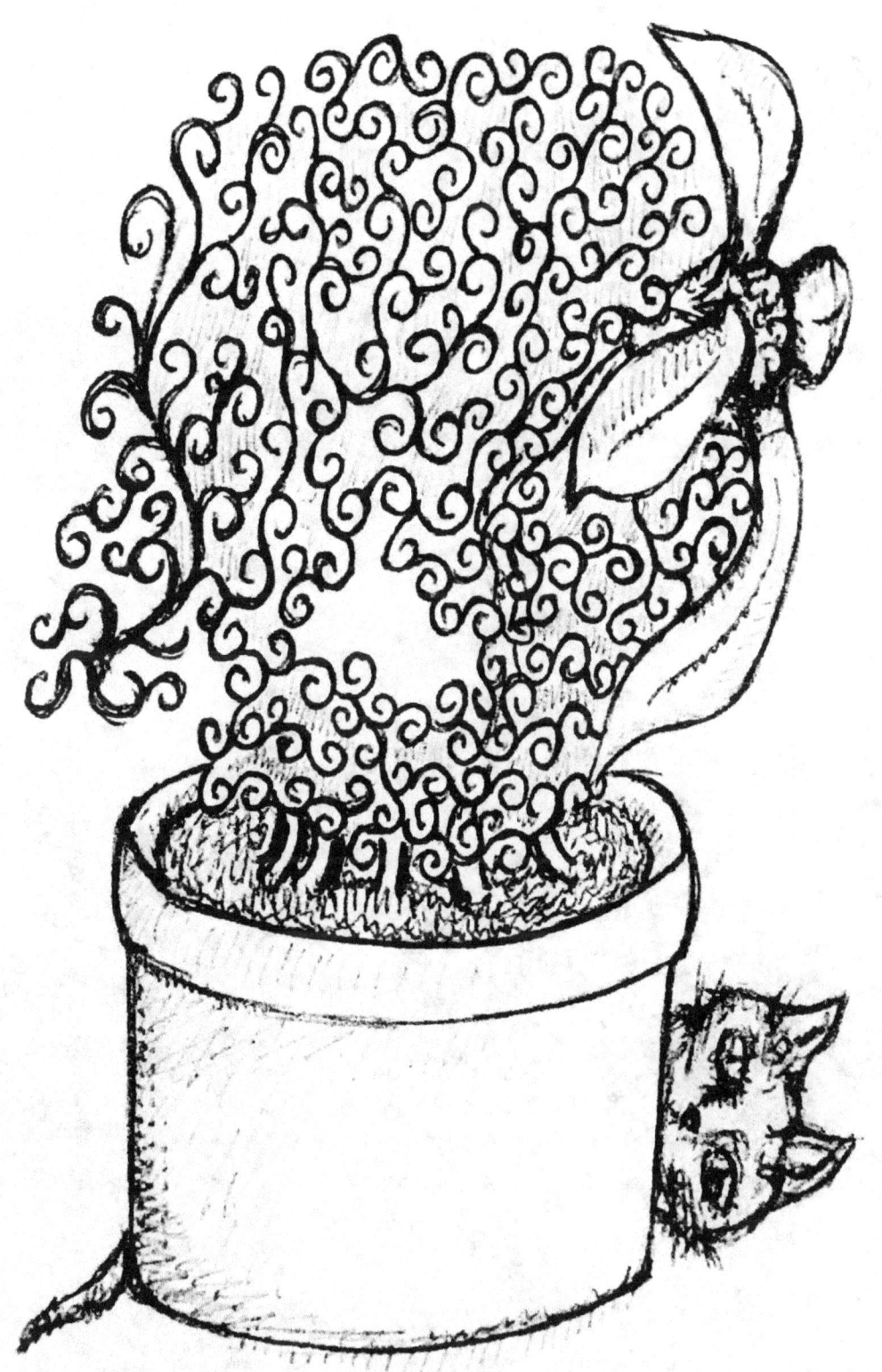

1

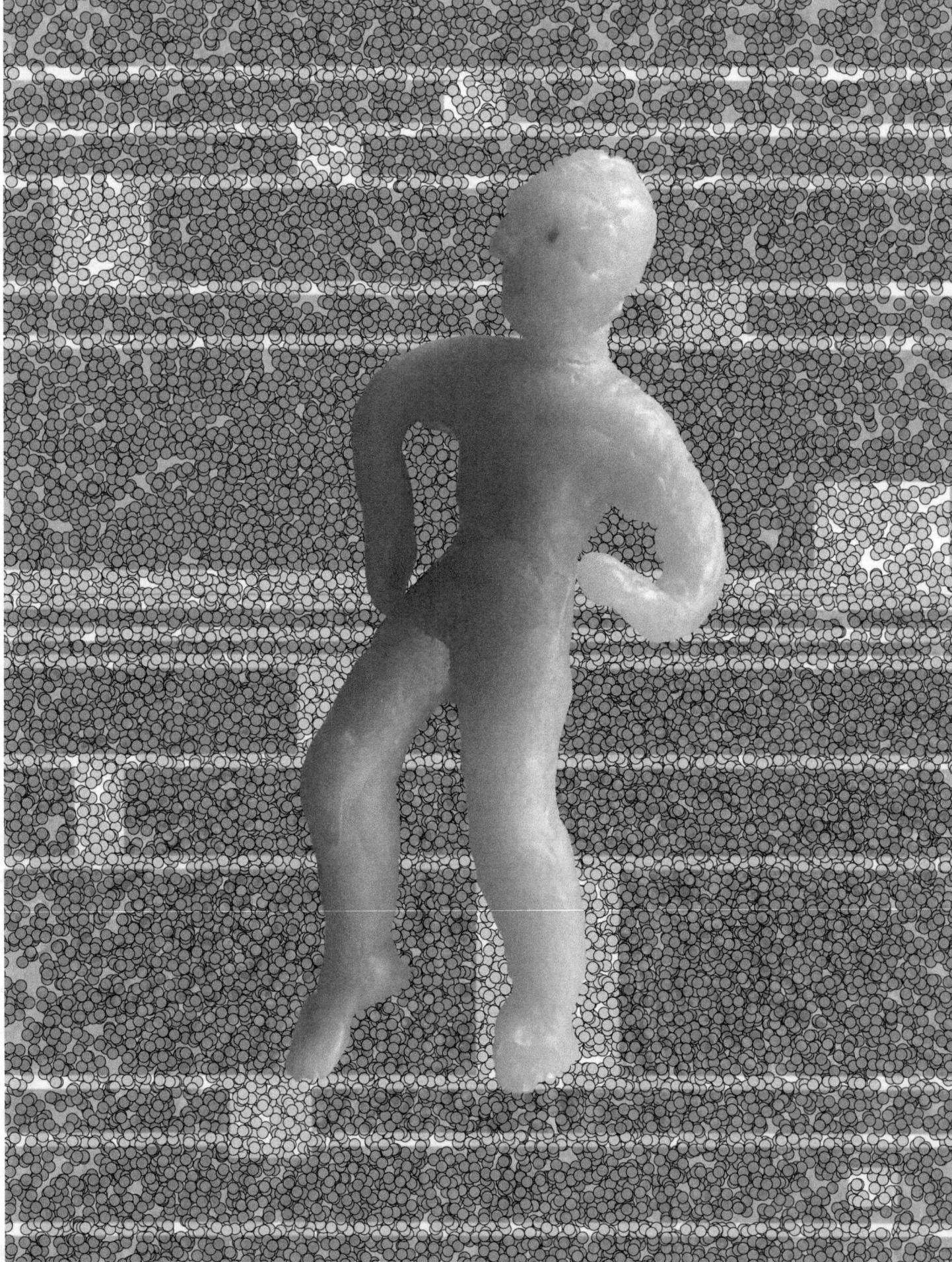

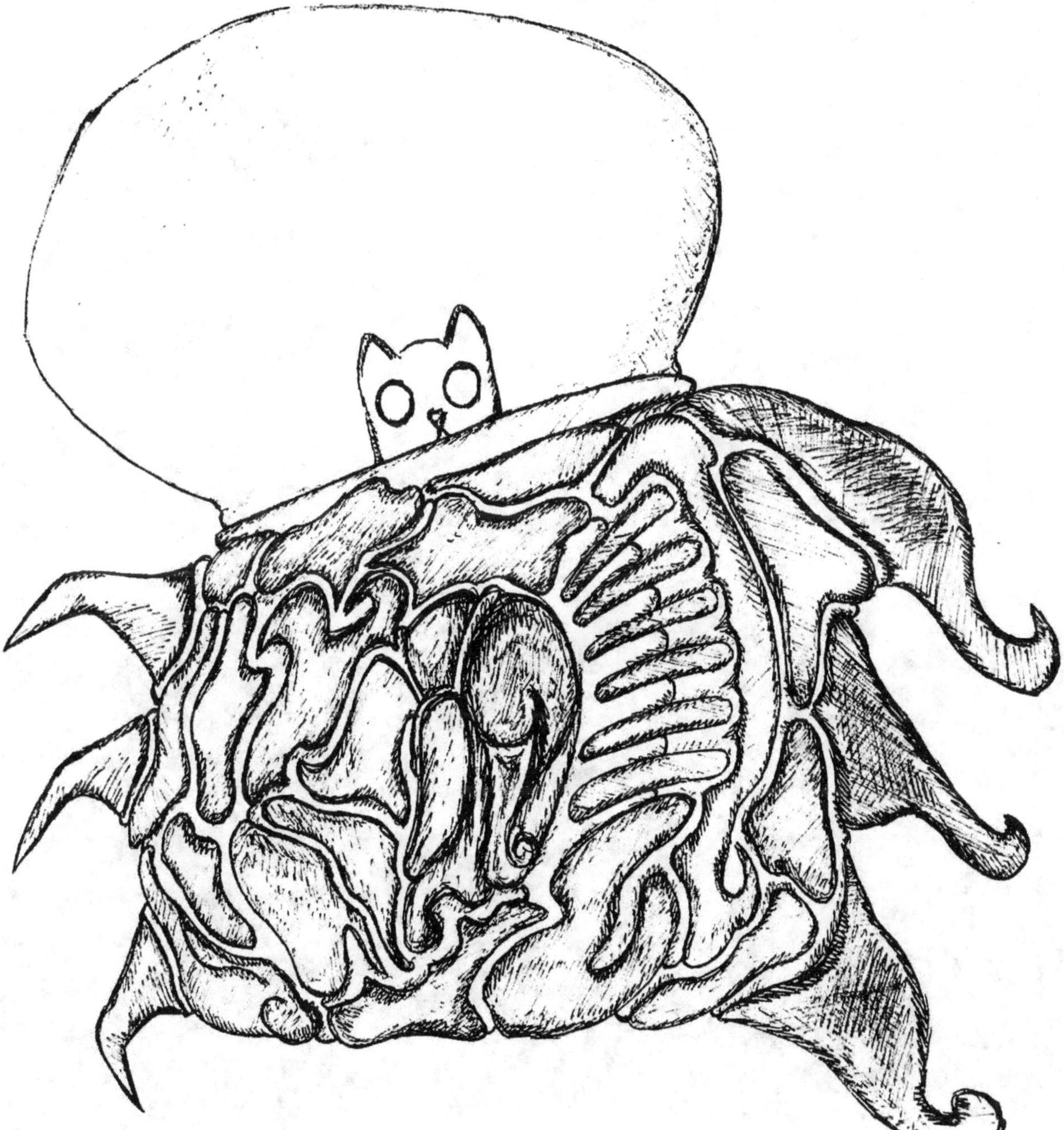

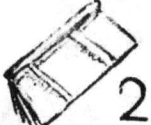

2

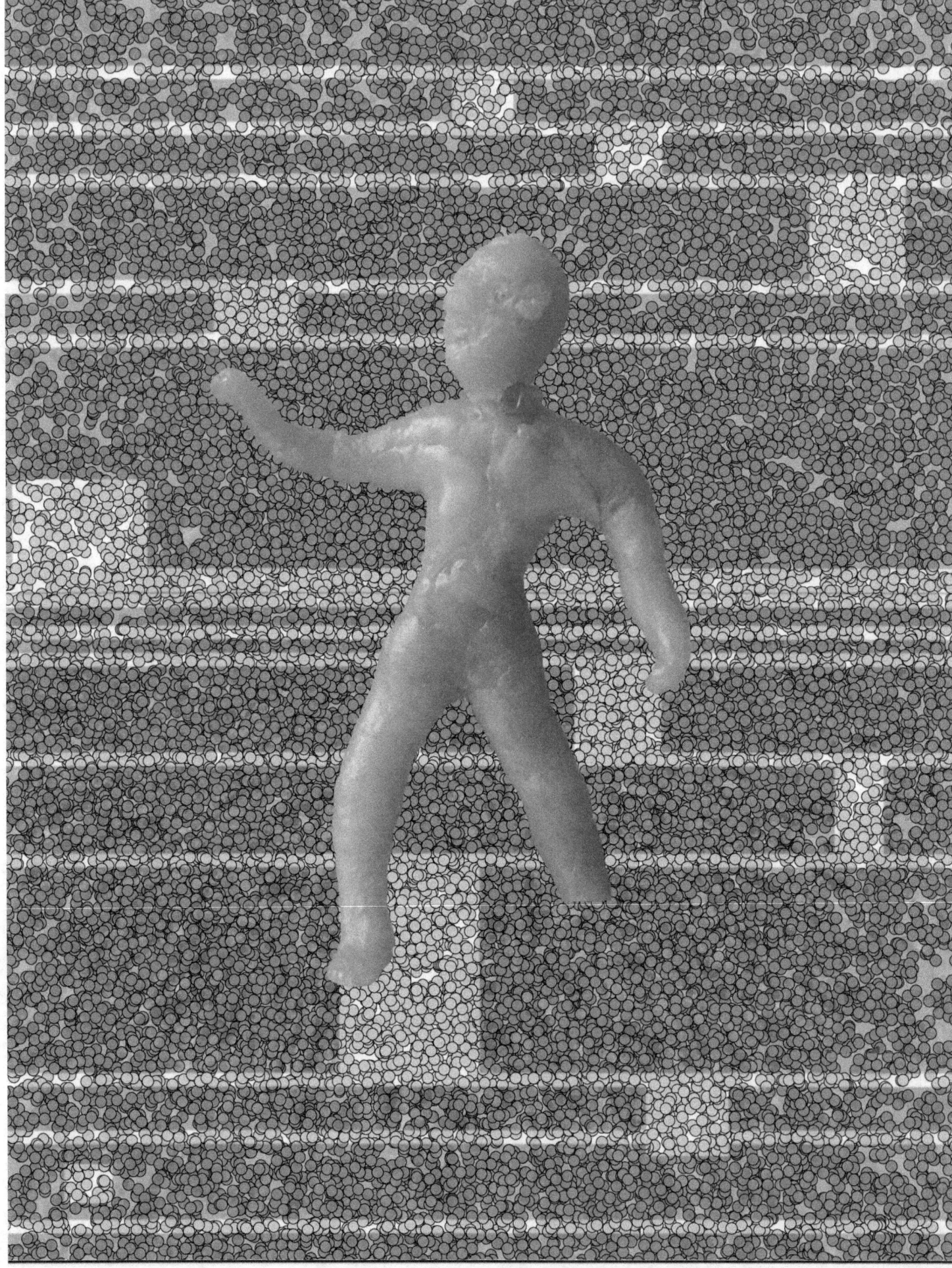

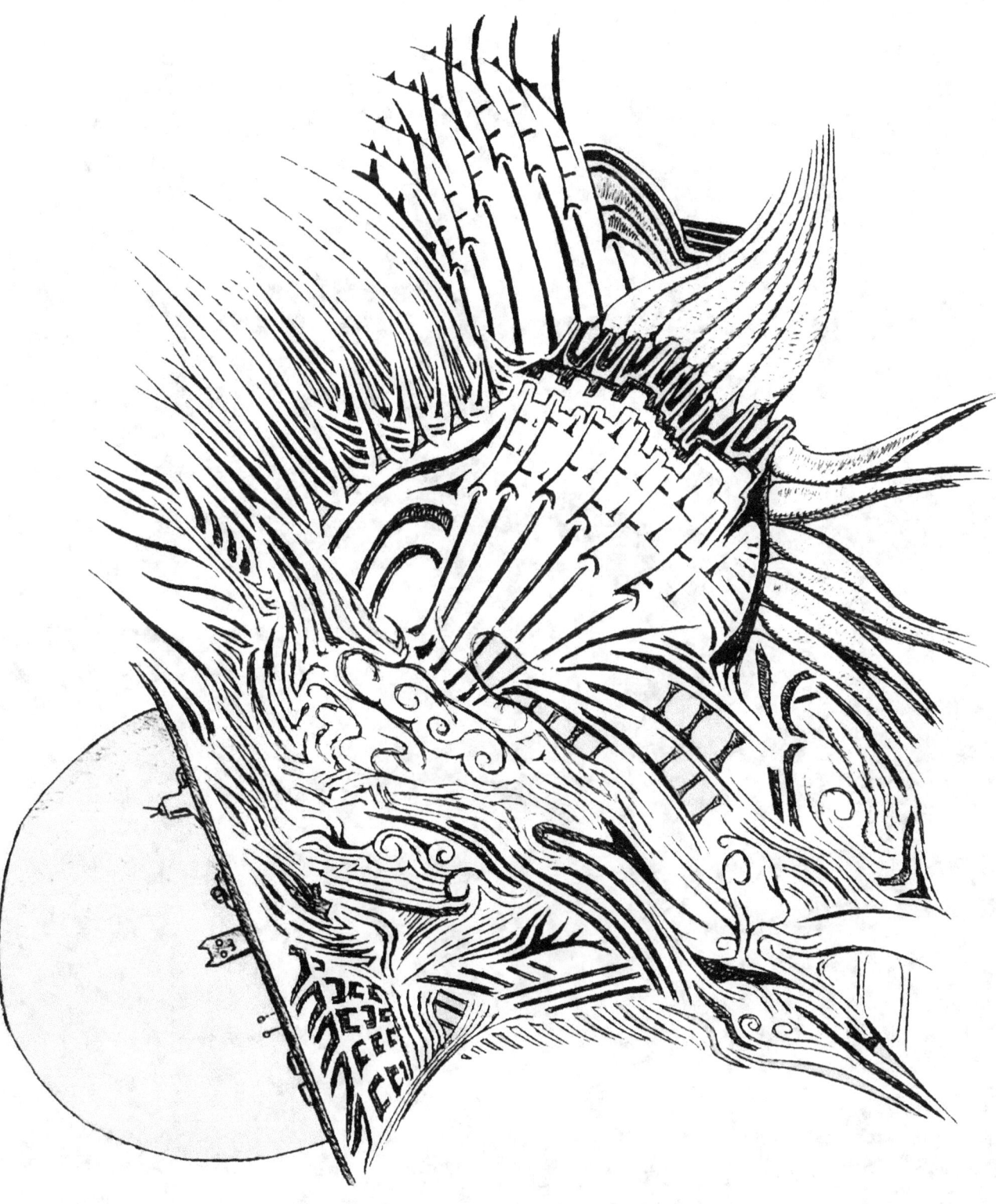

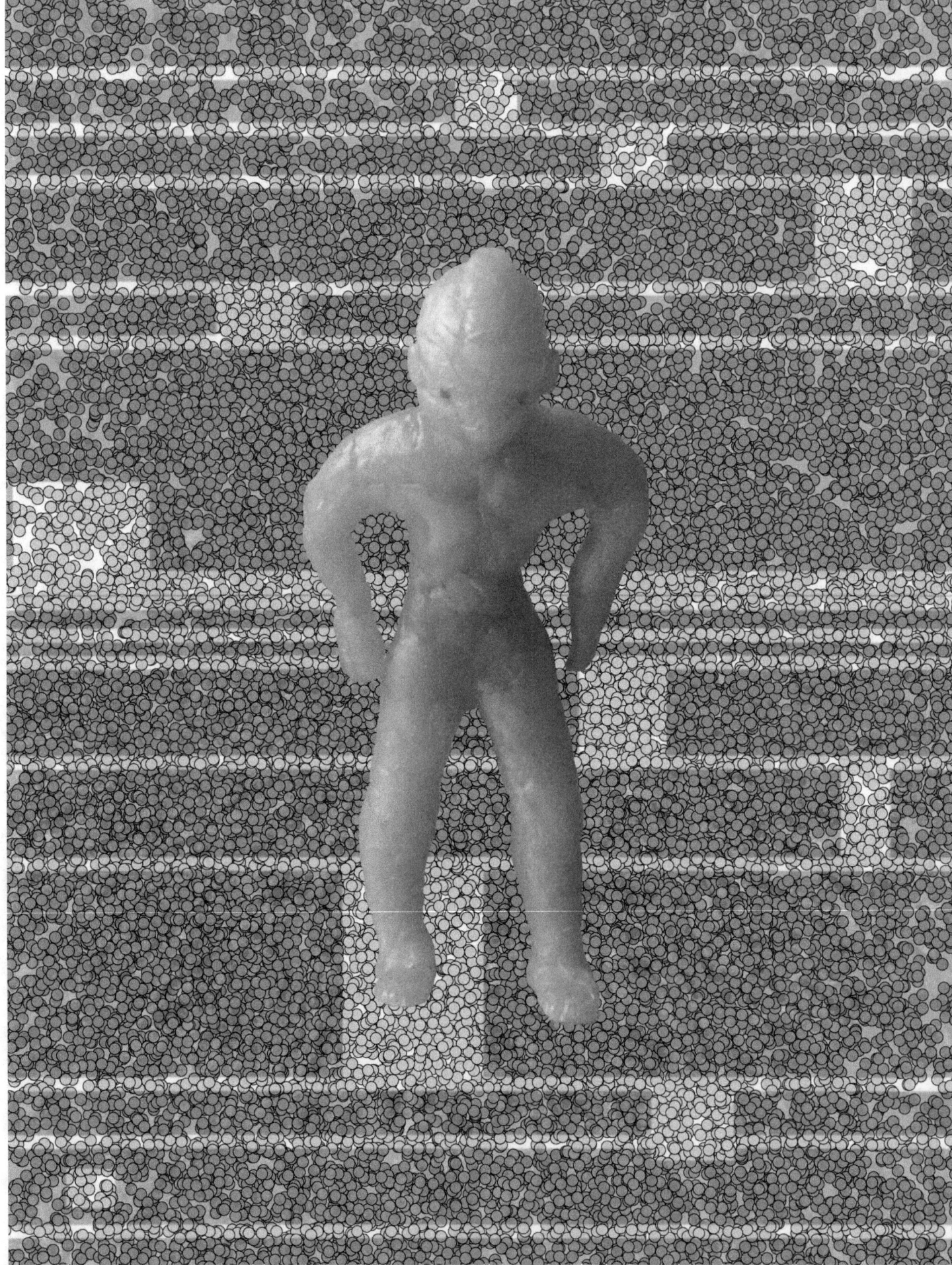

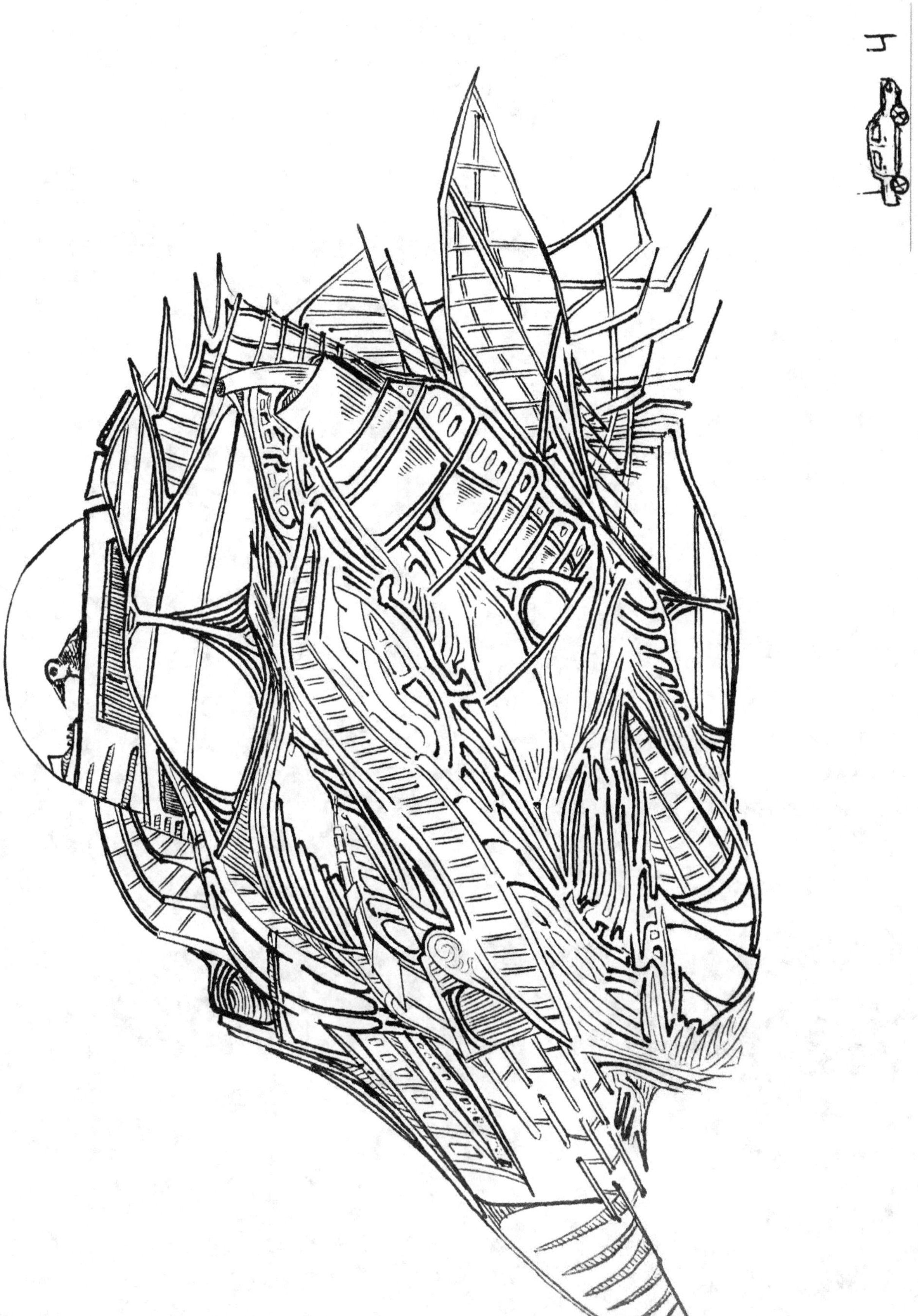

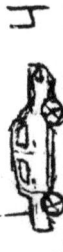

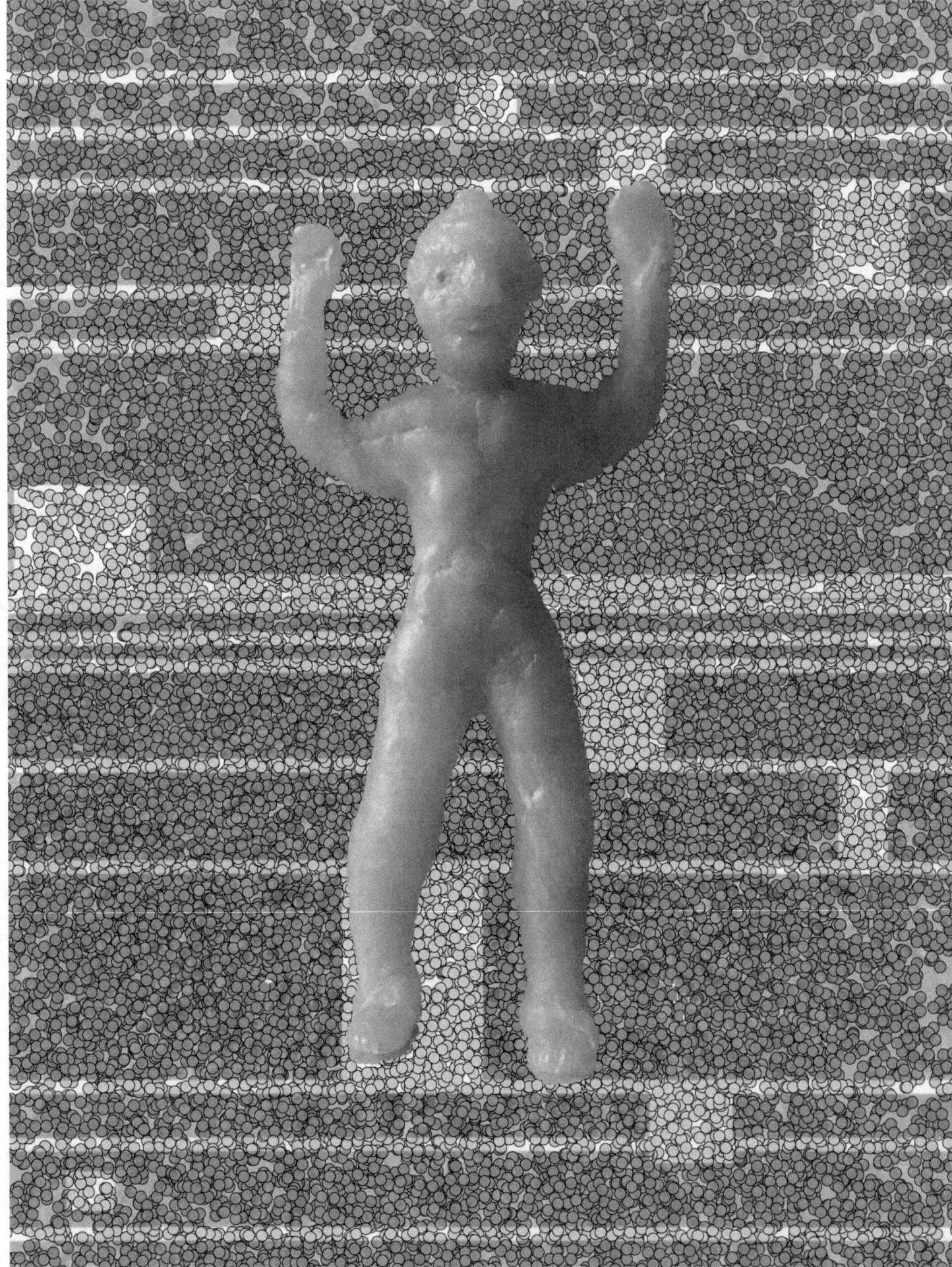

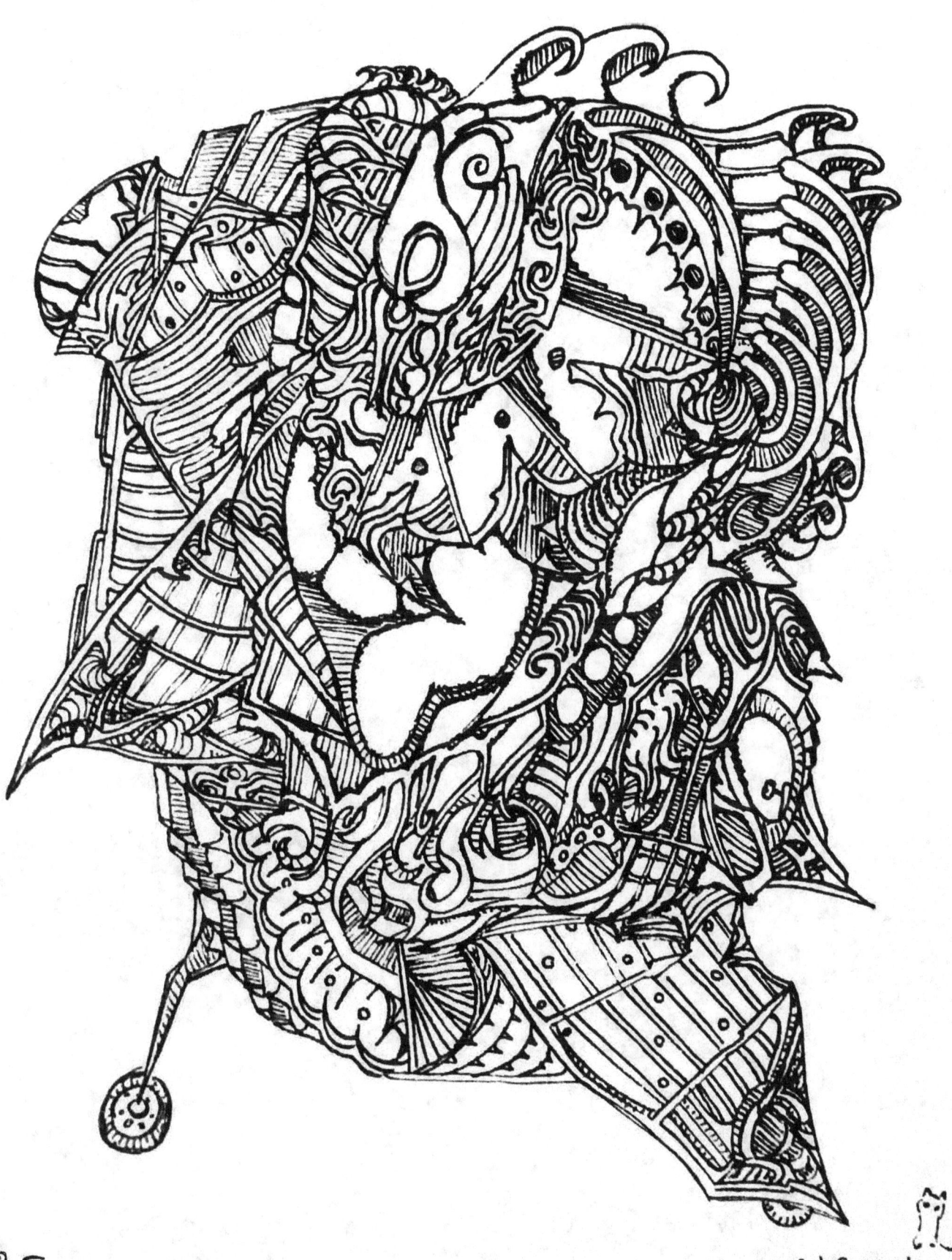

5

Cat for scale

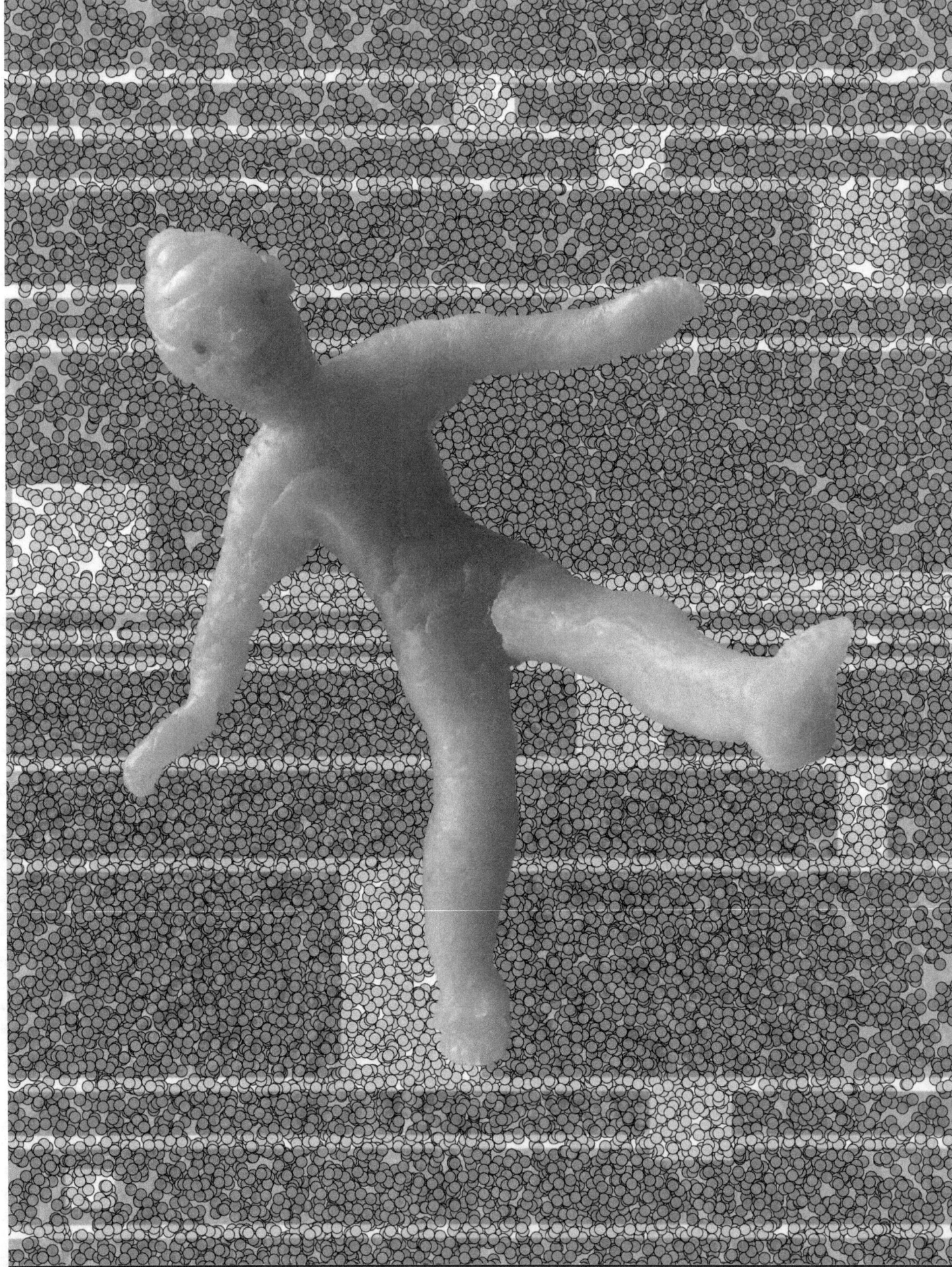

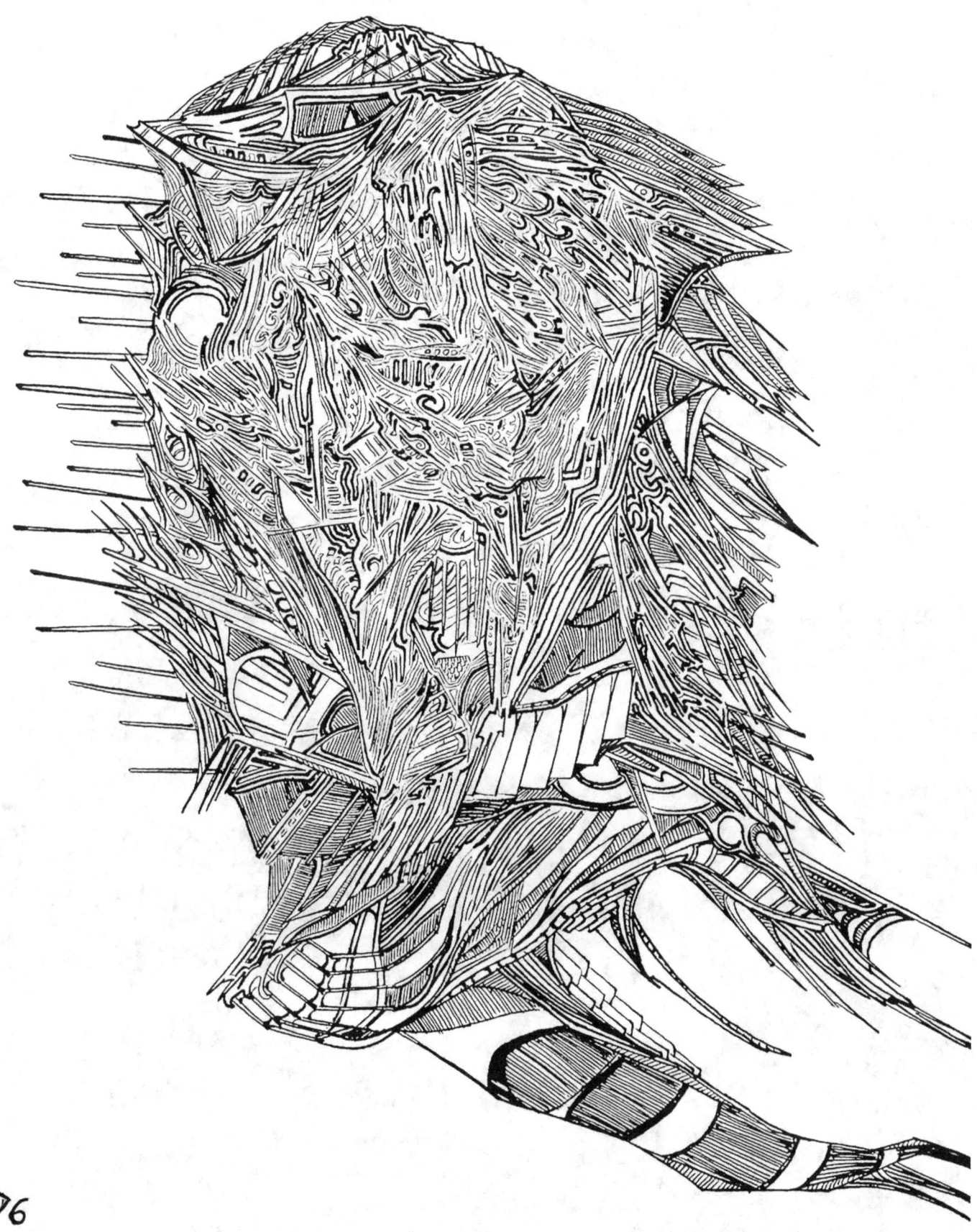

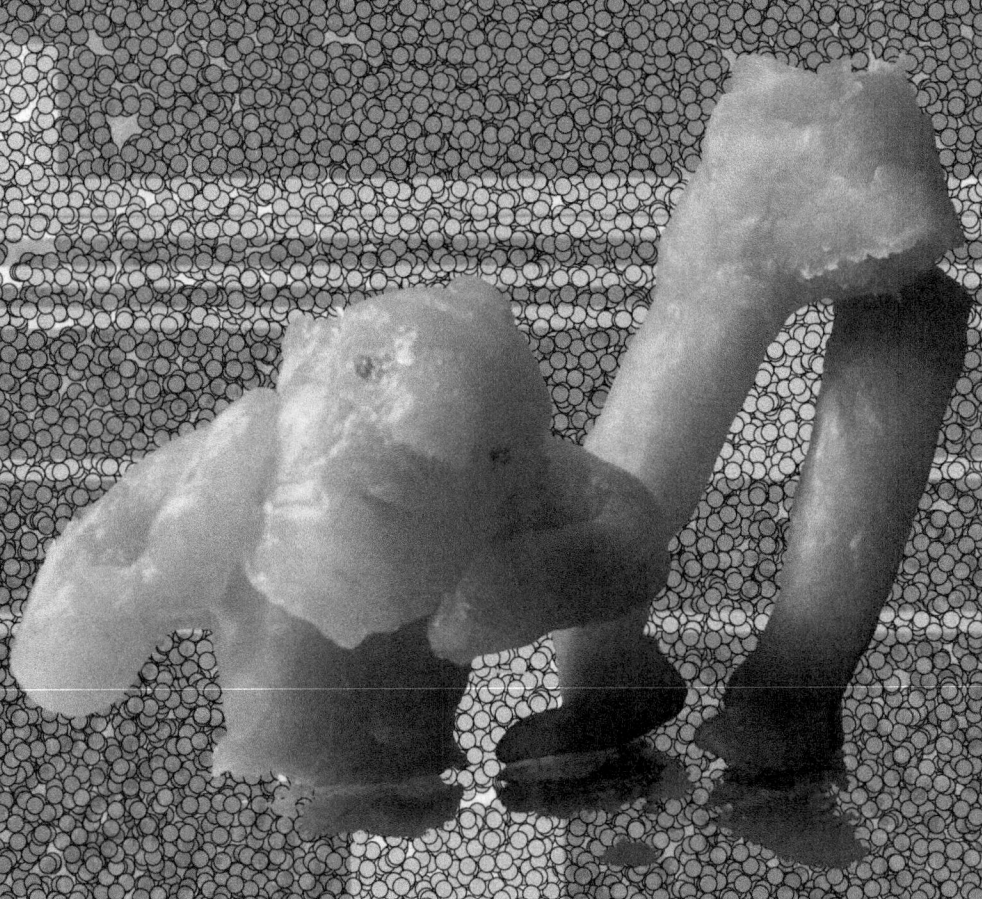

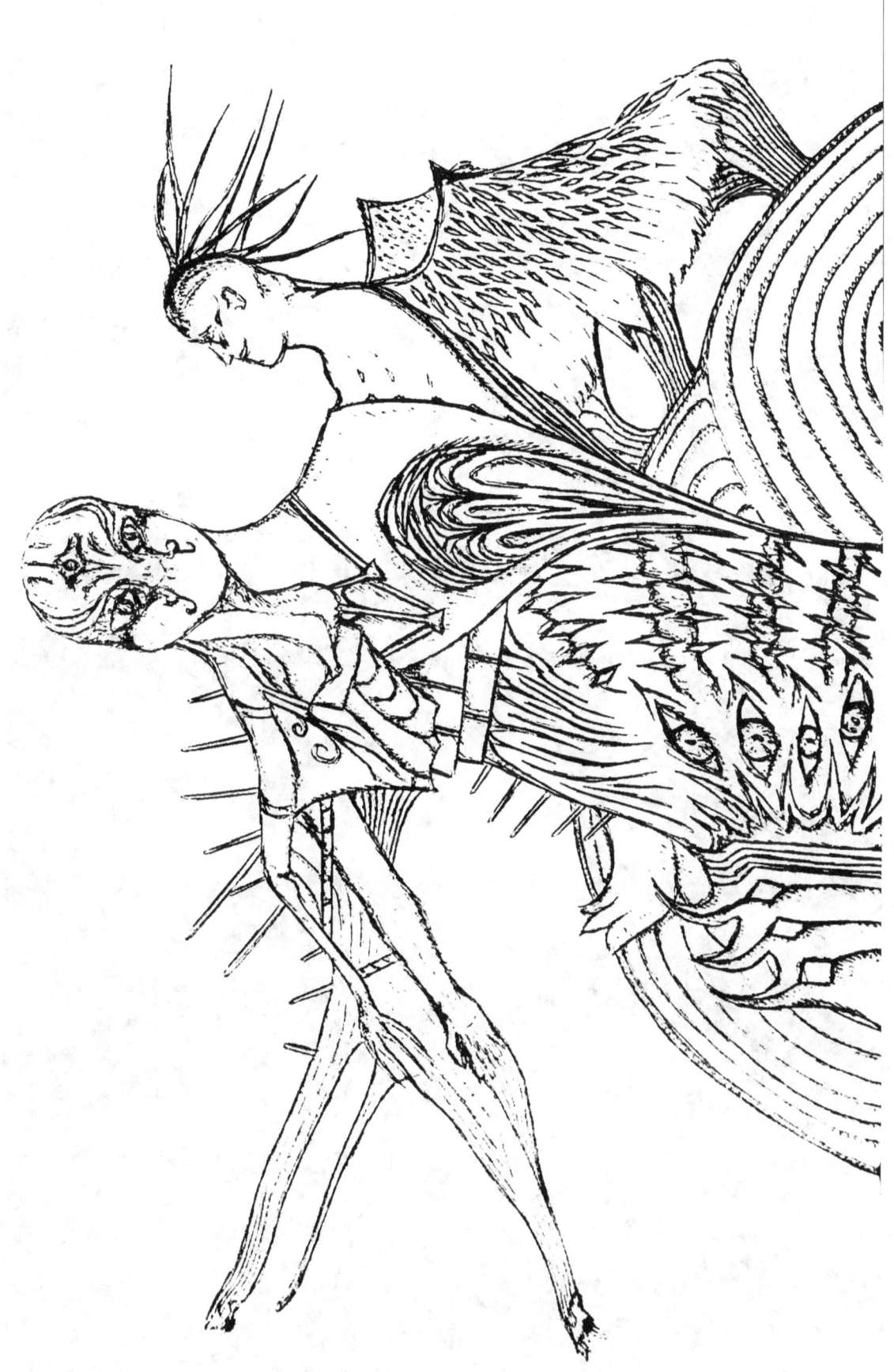

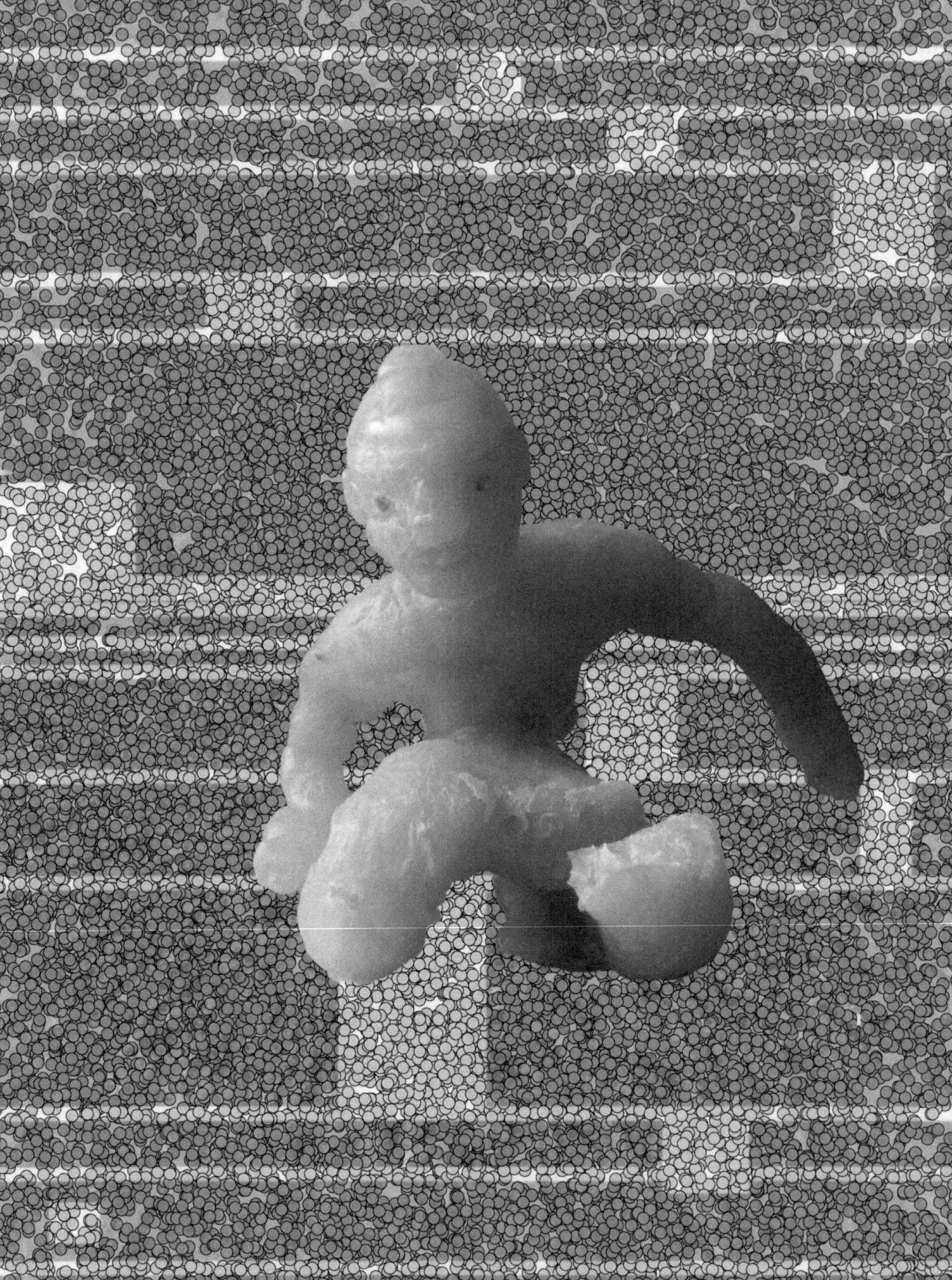

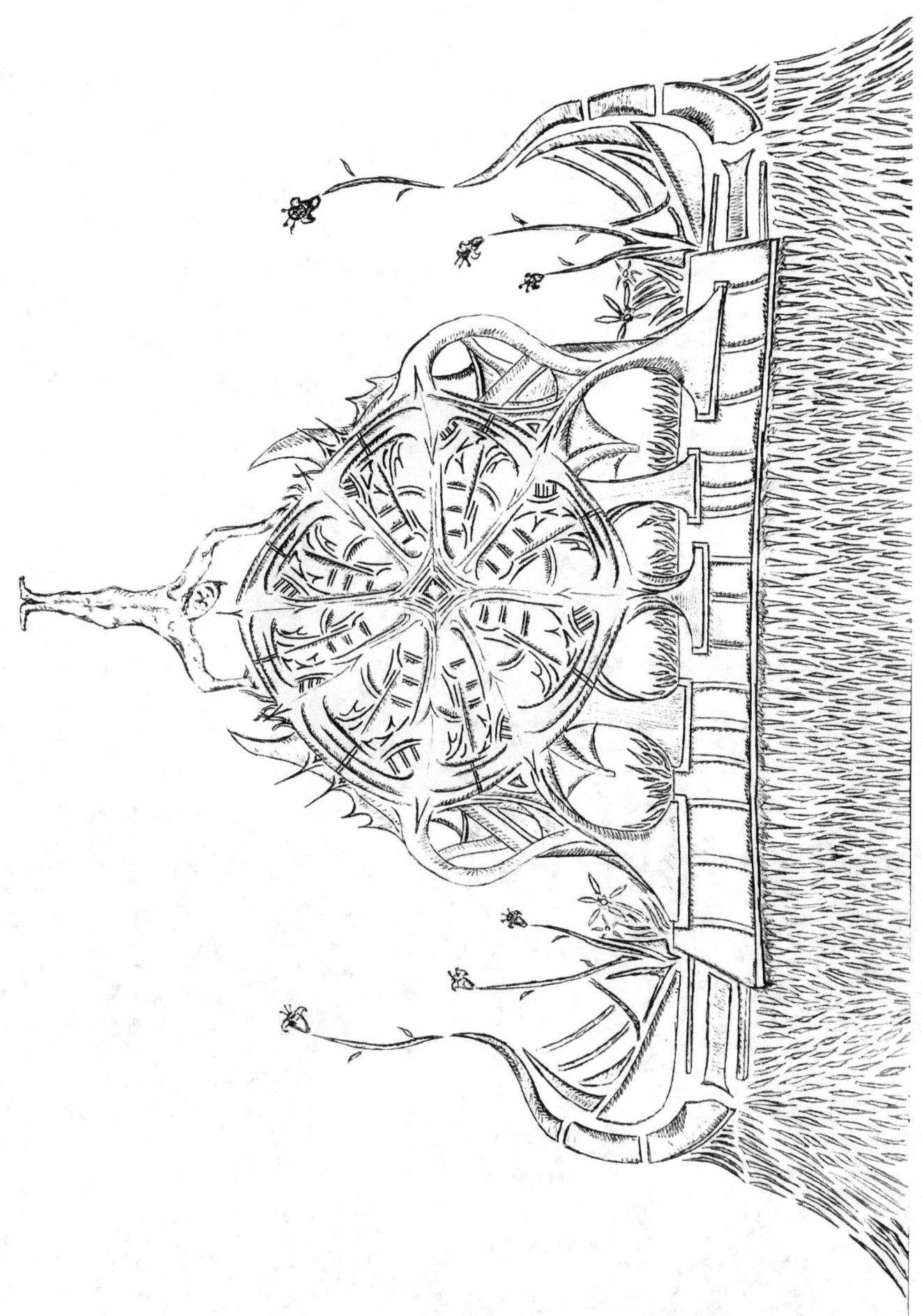

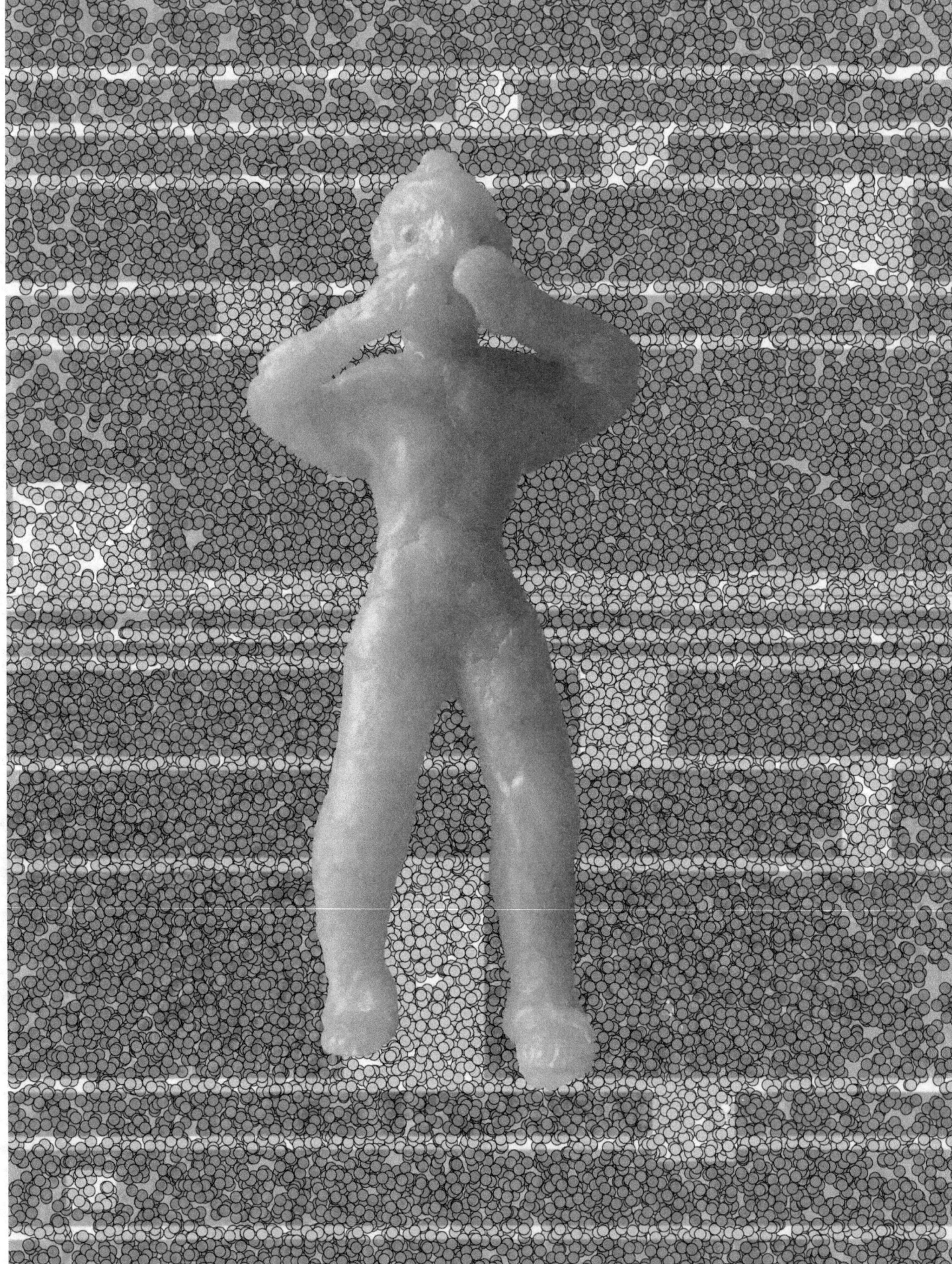

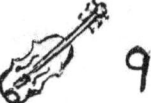

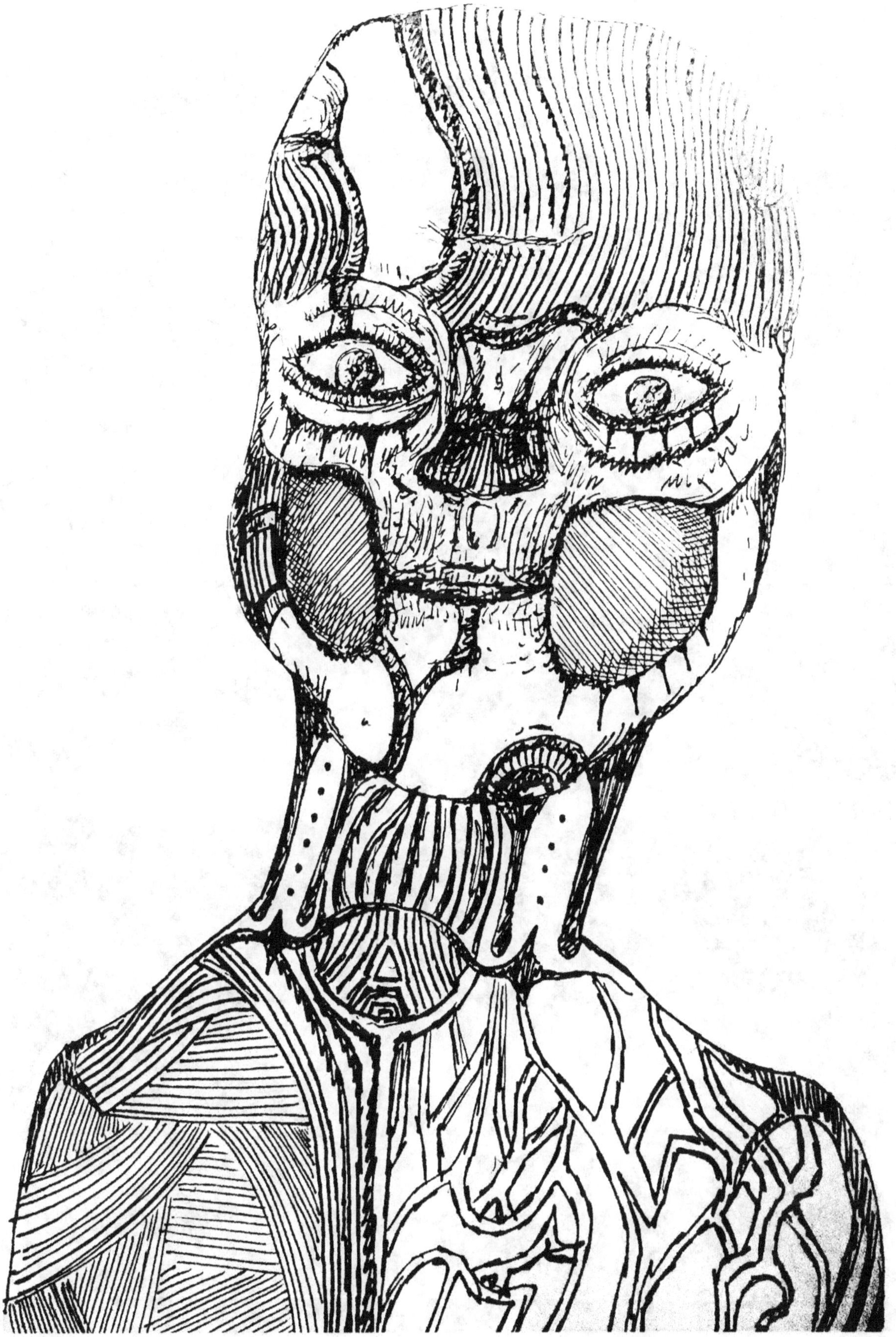

9

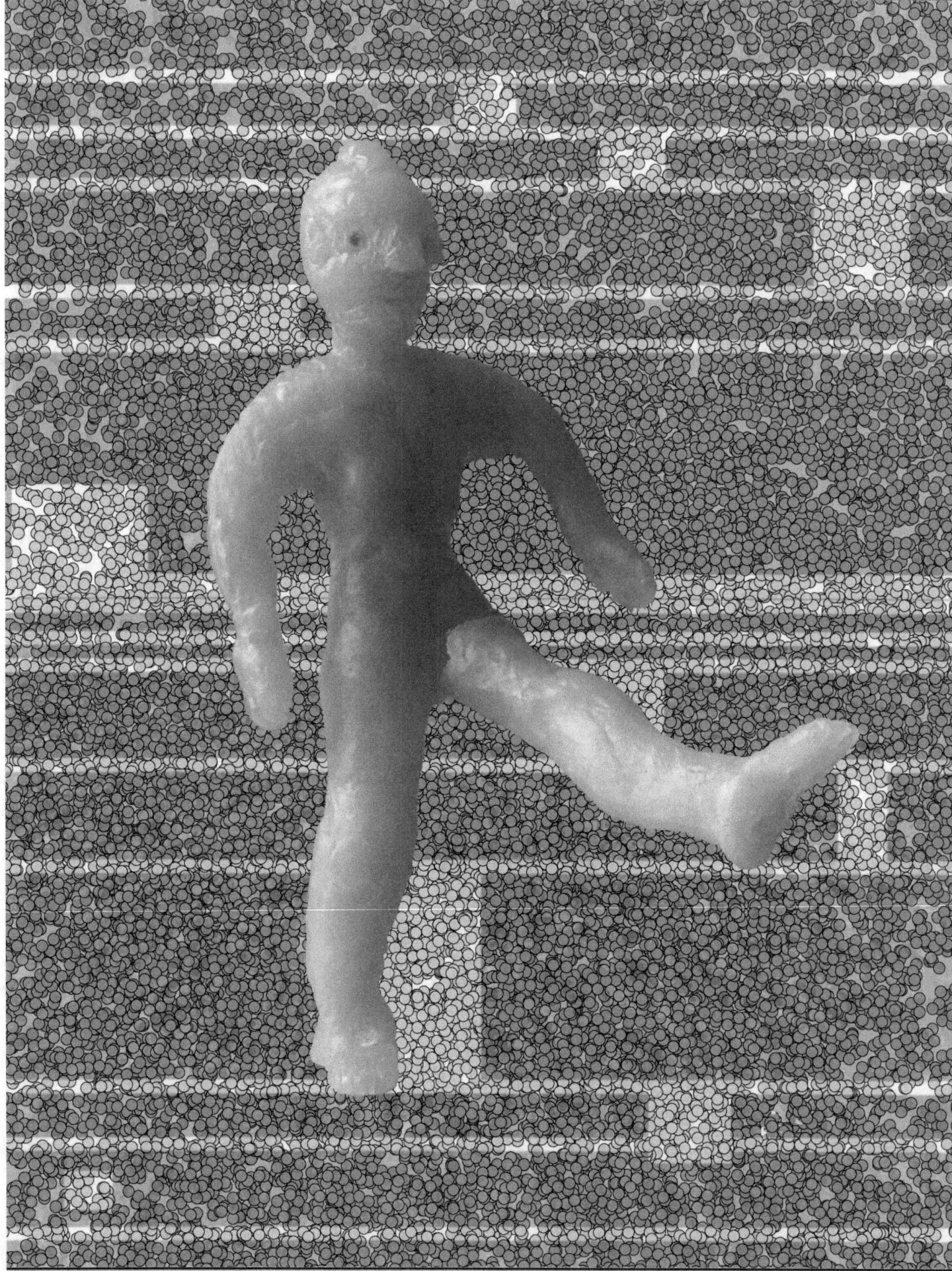

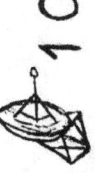

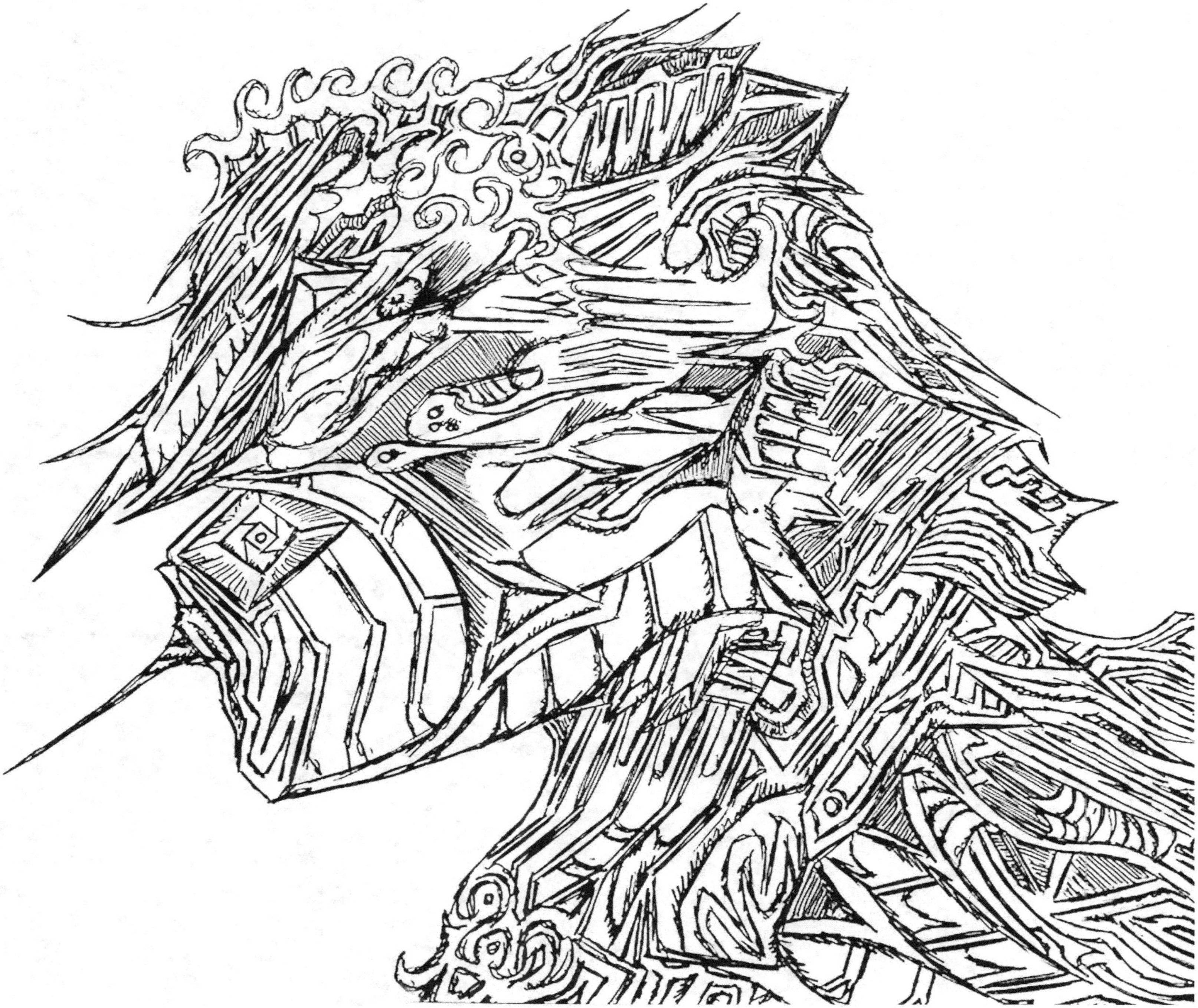

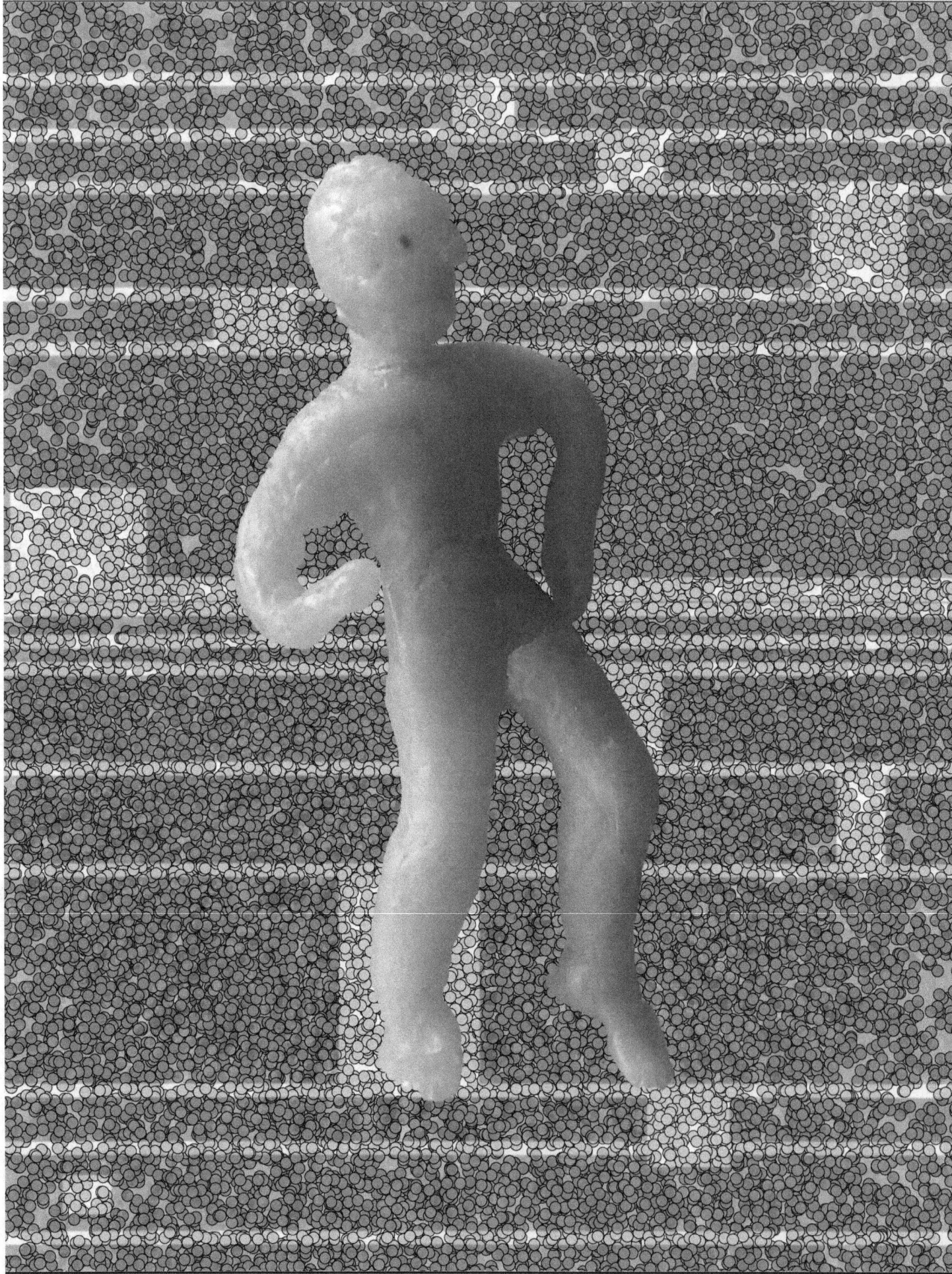

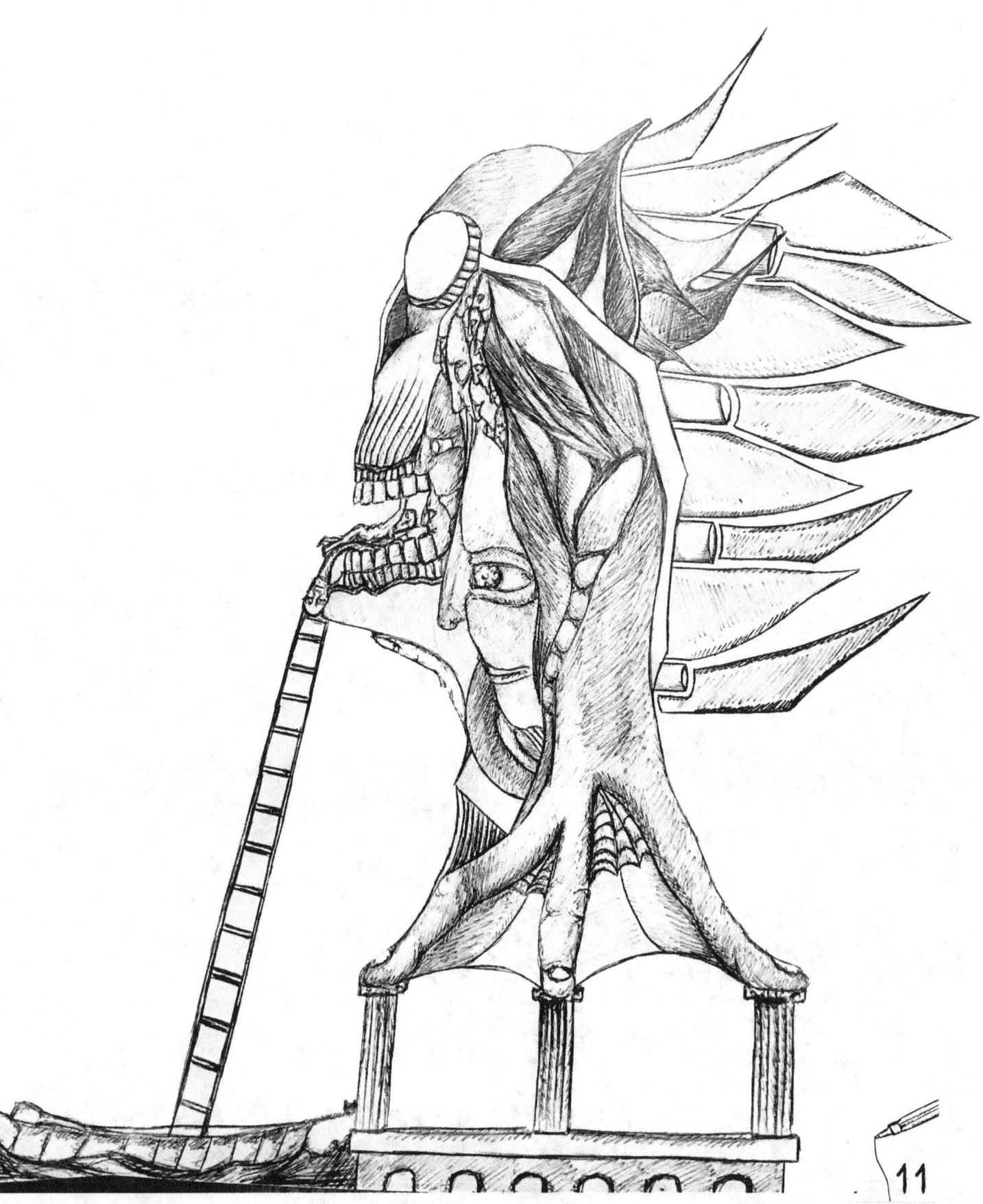

11

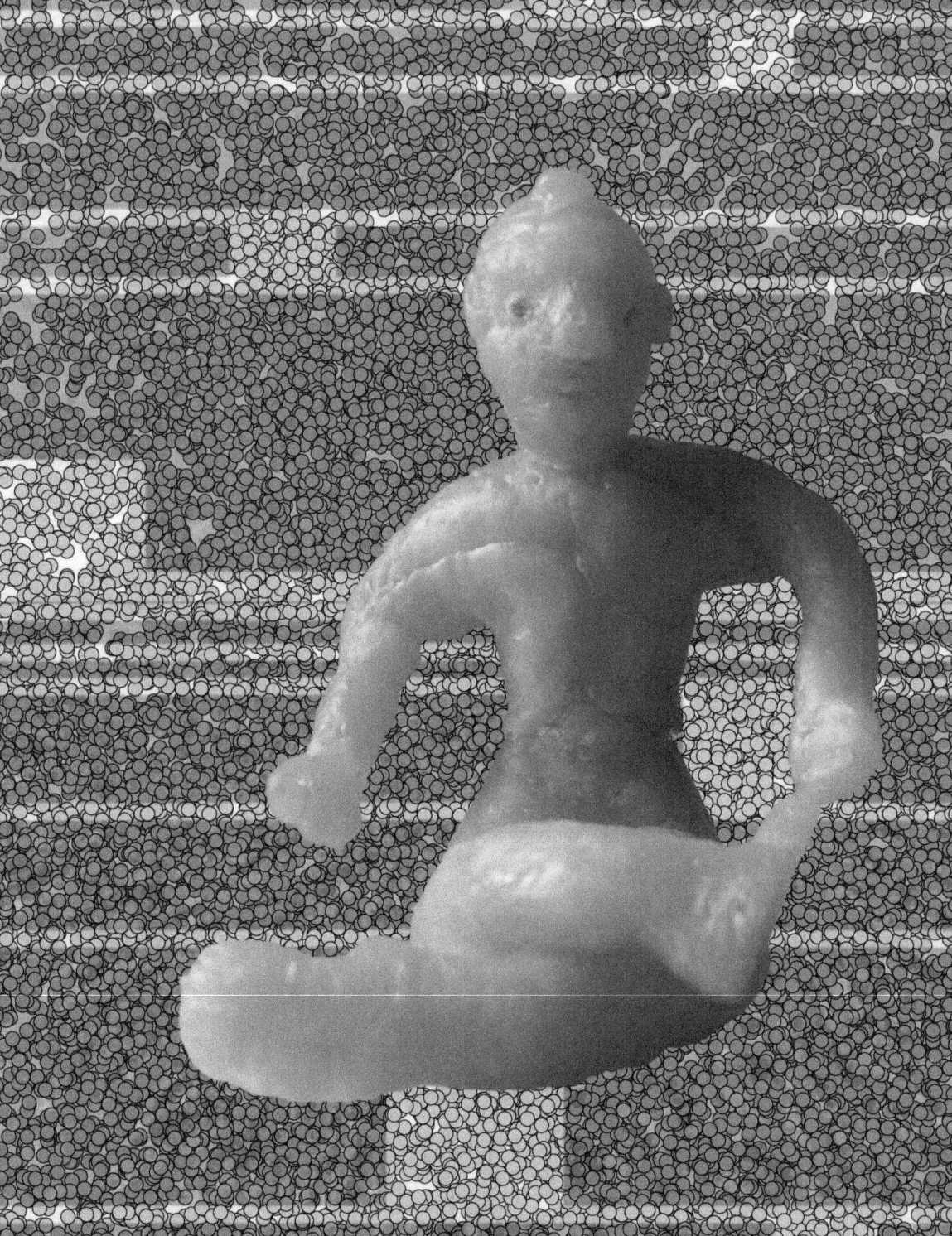

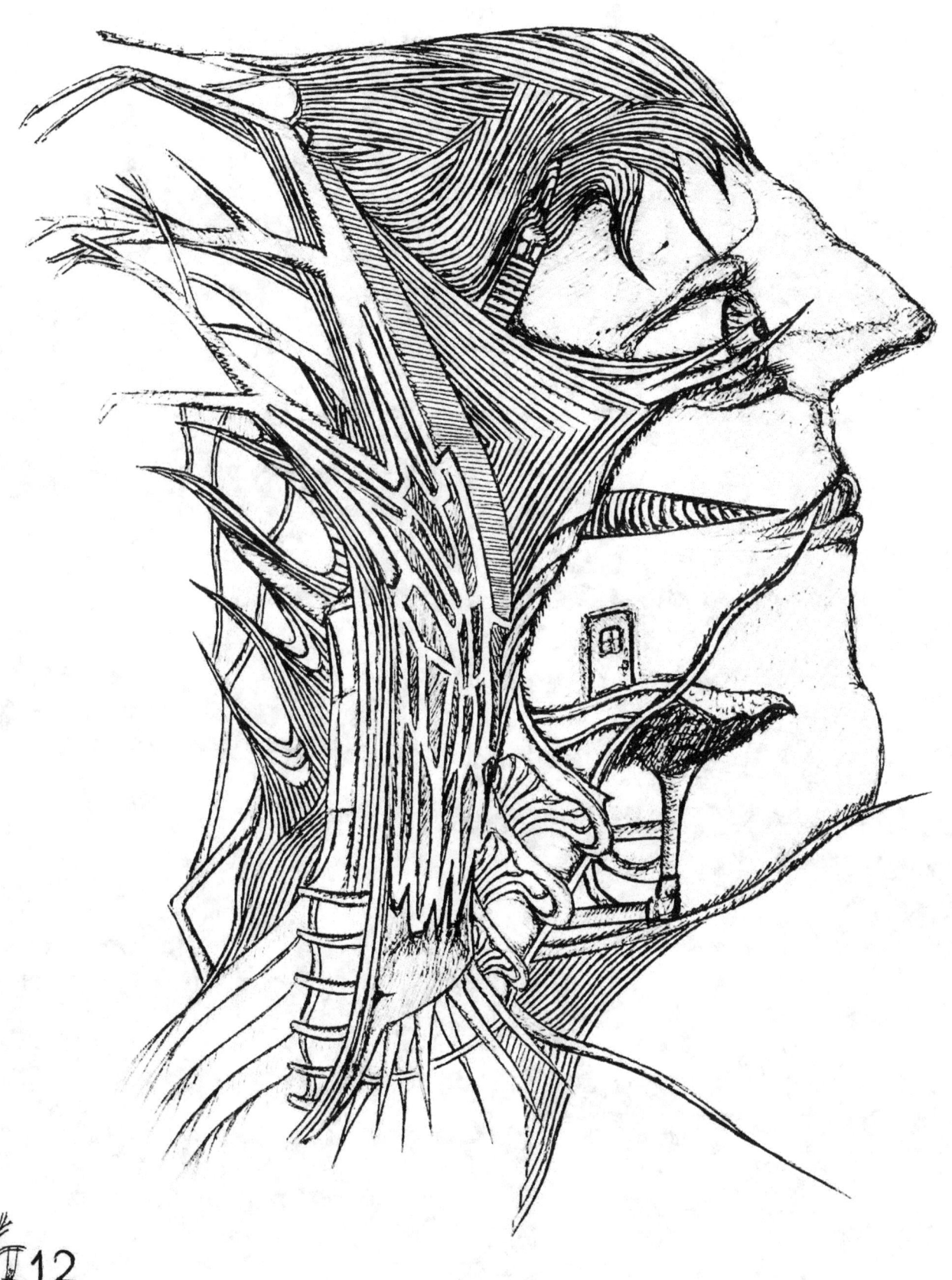

12

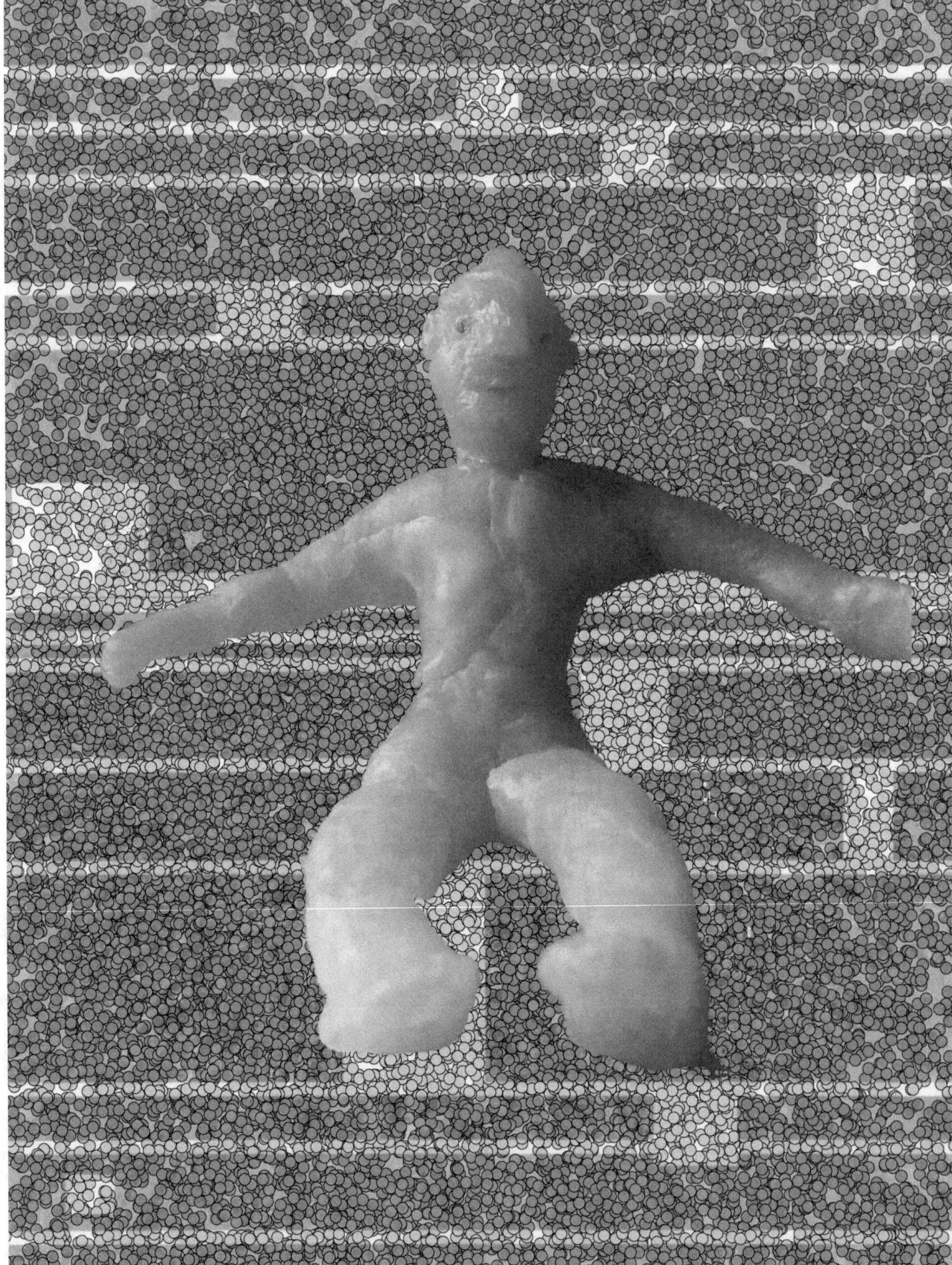

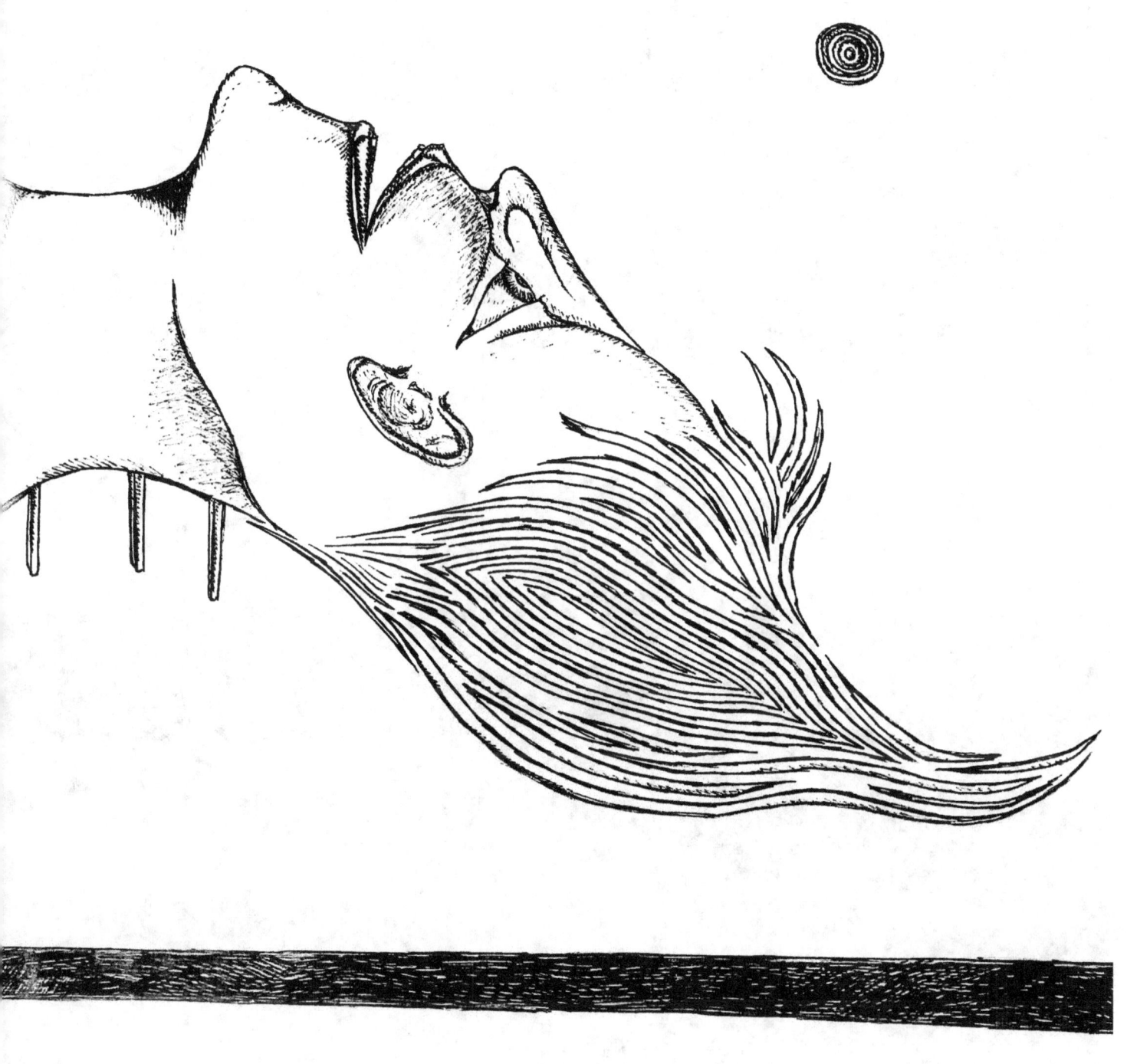

13

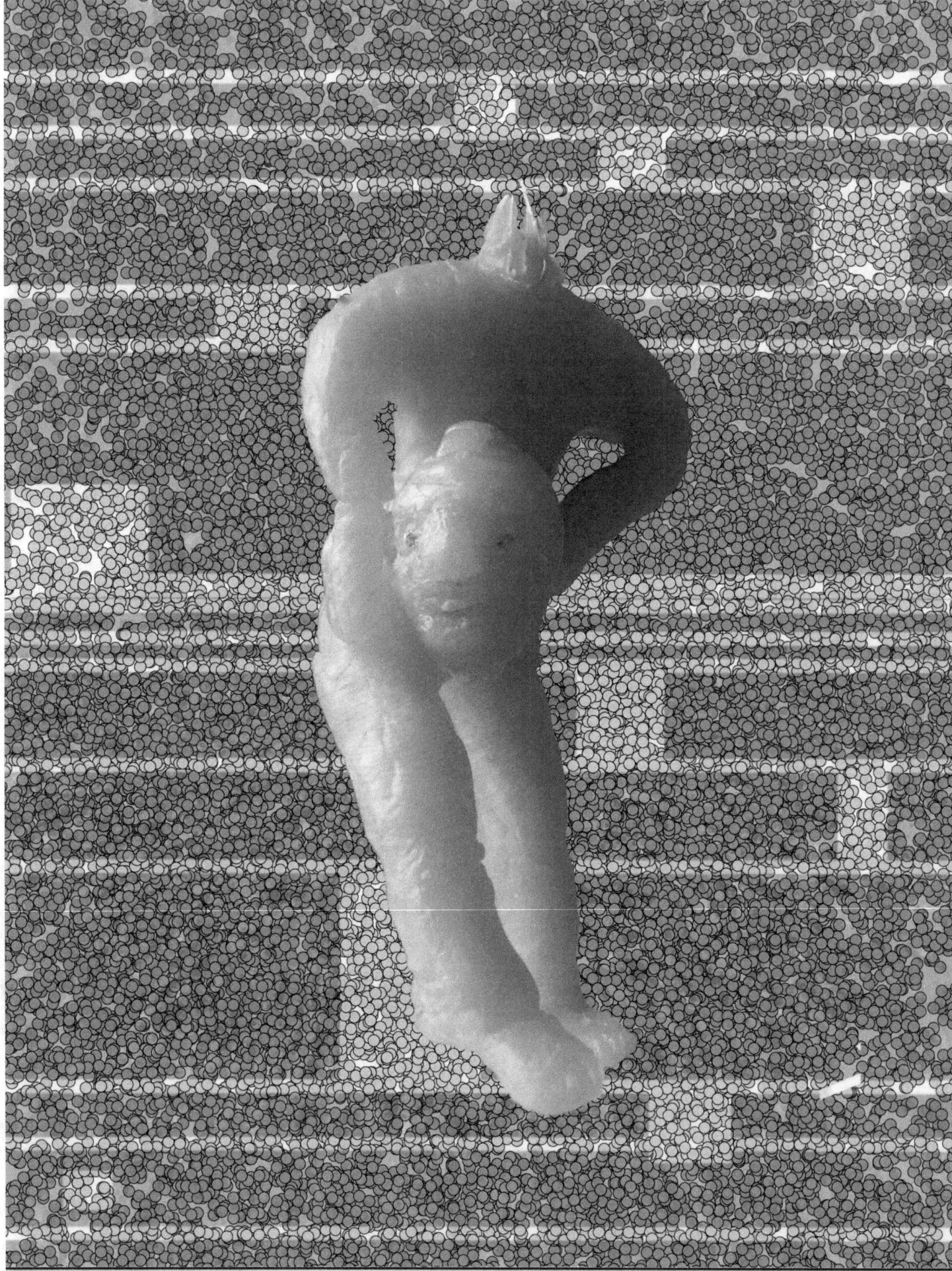

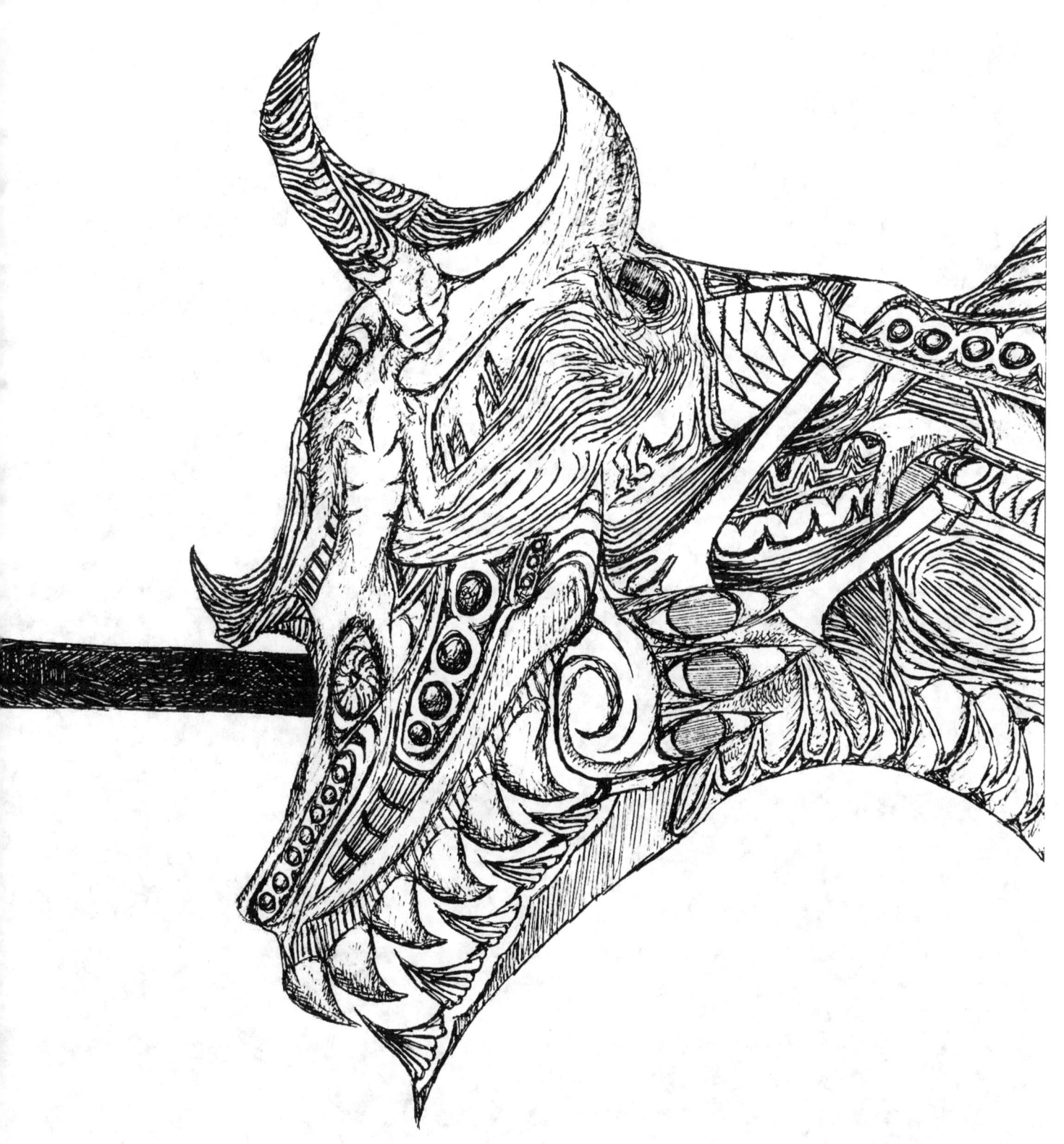

14

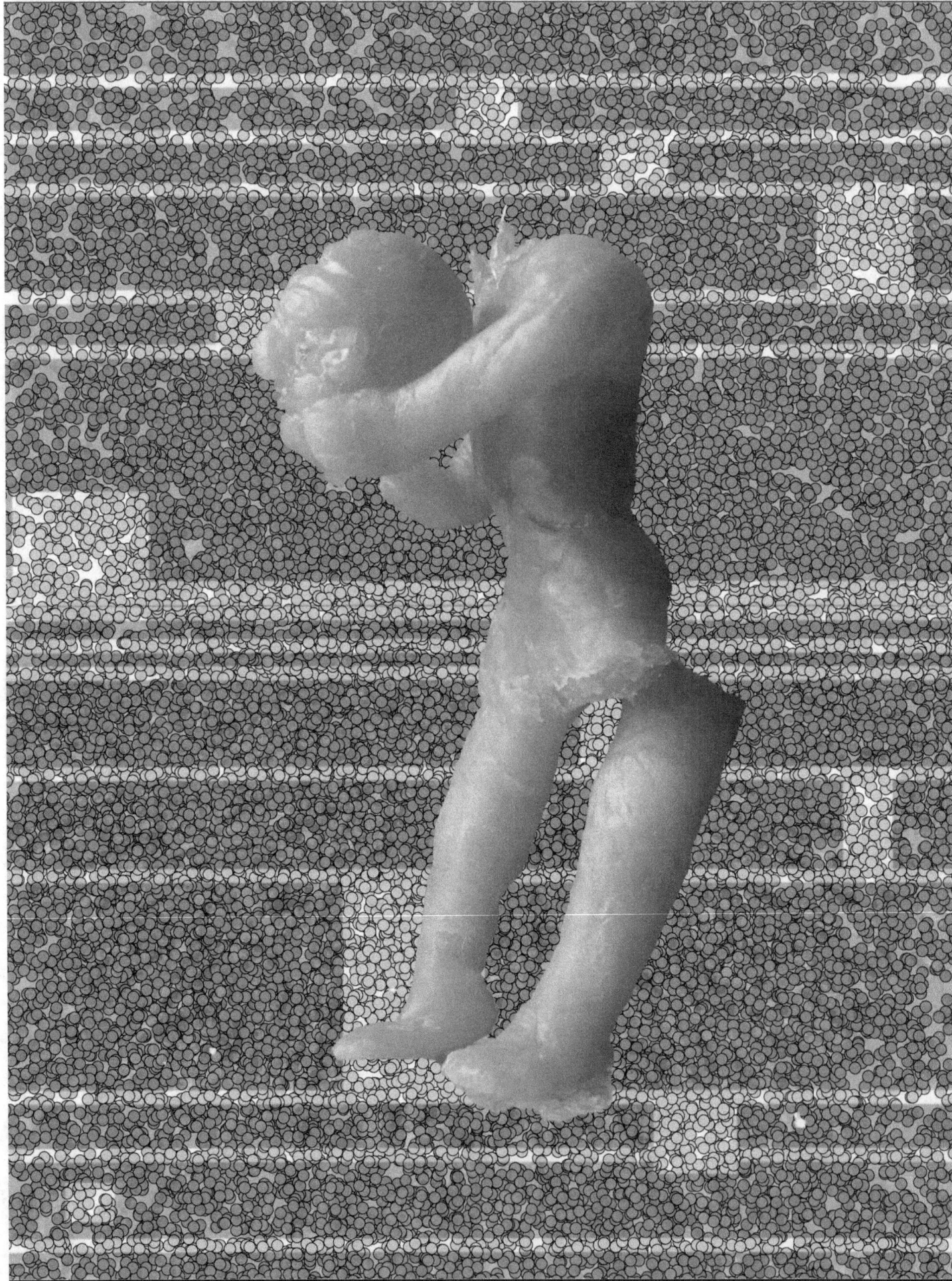

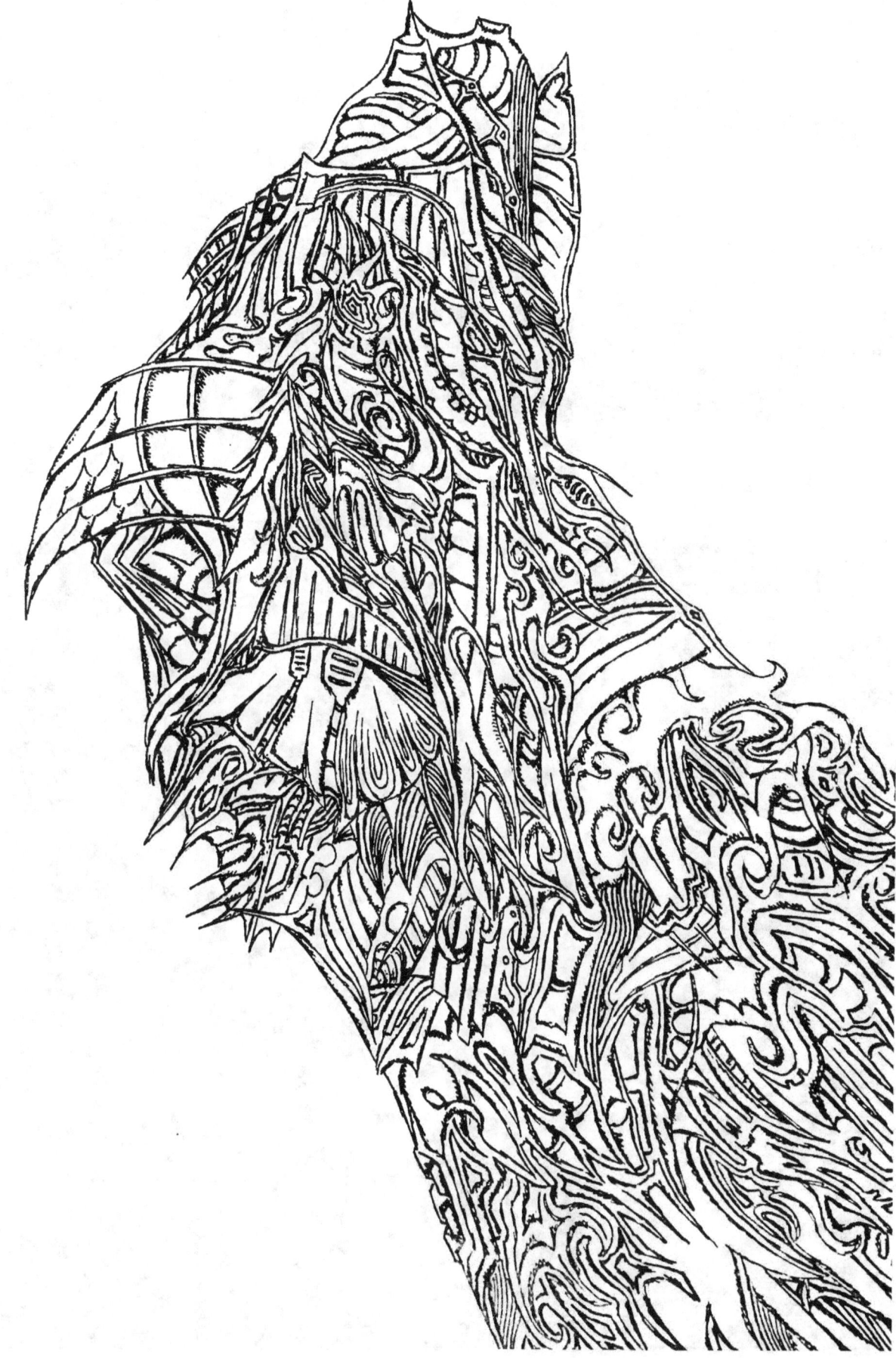

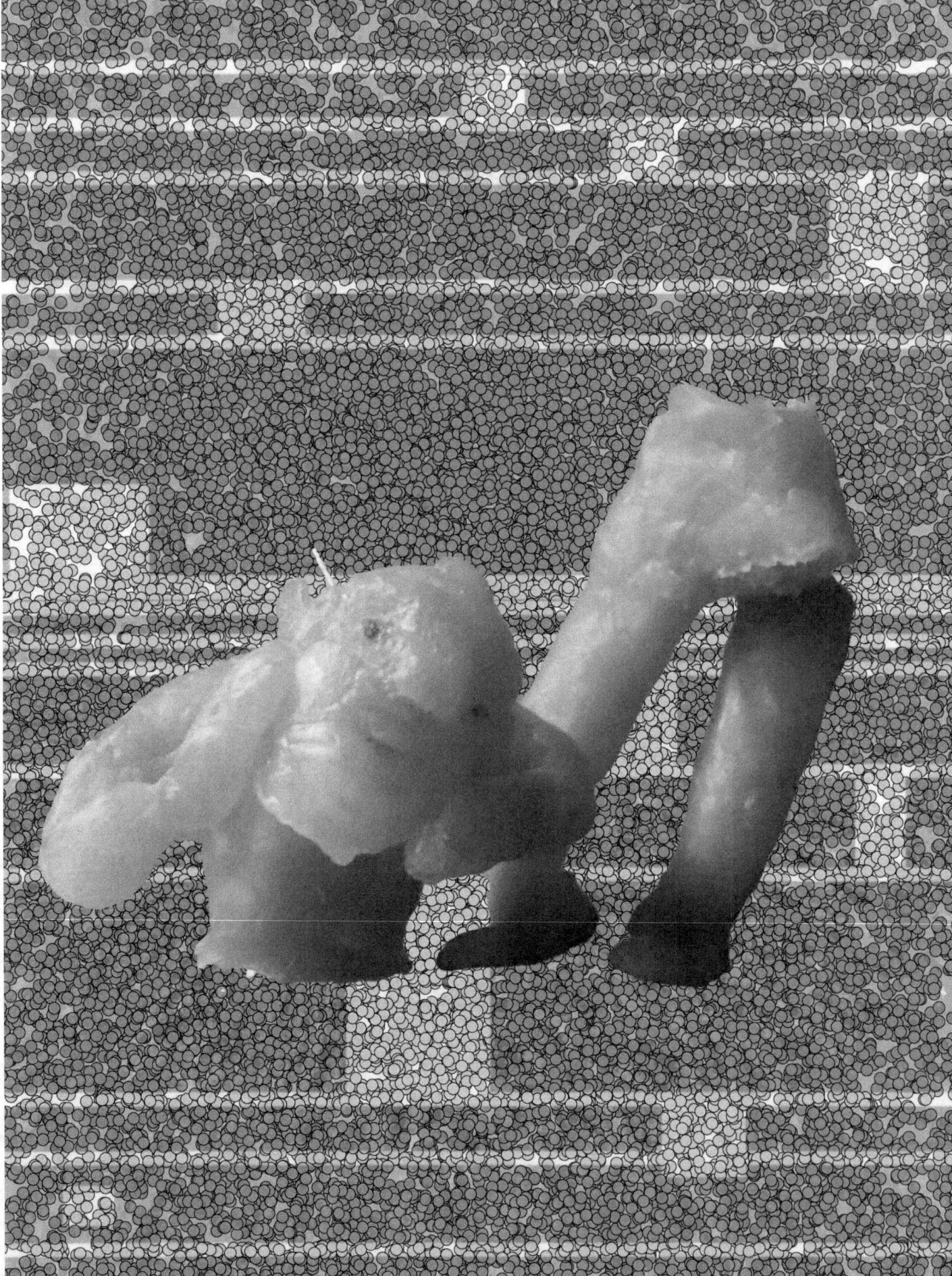

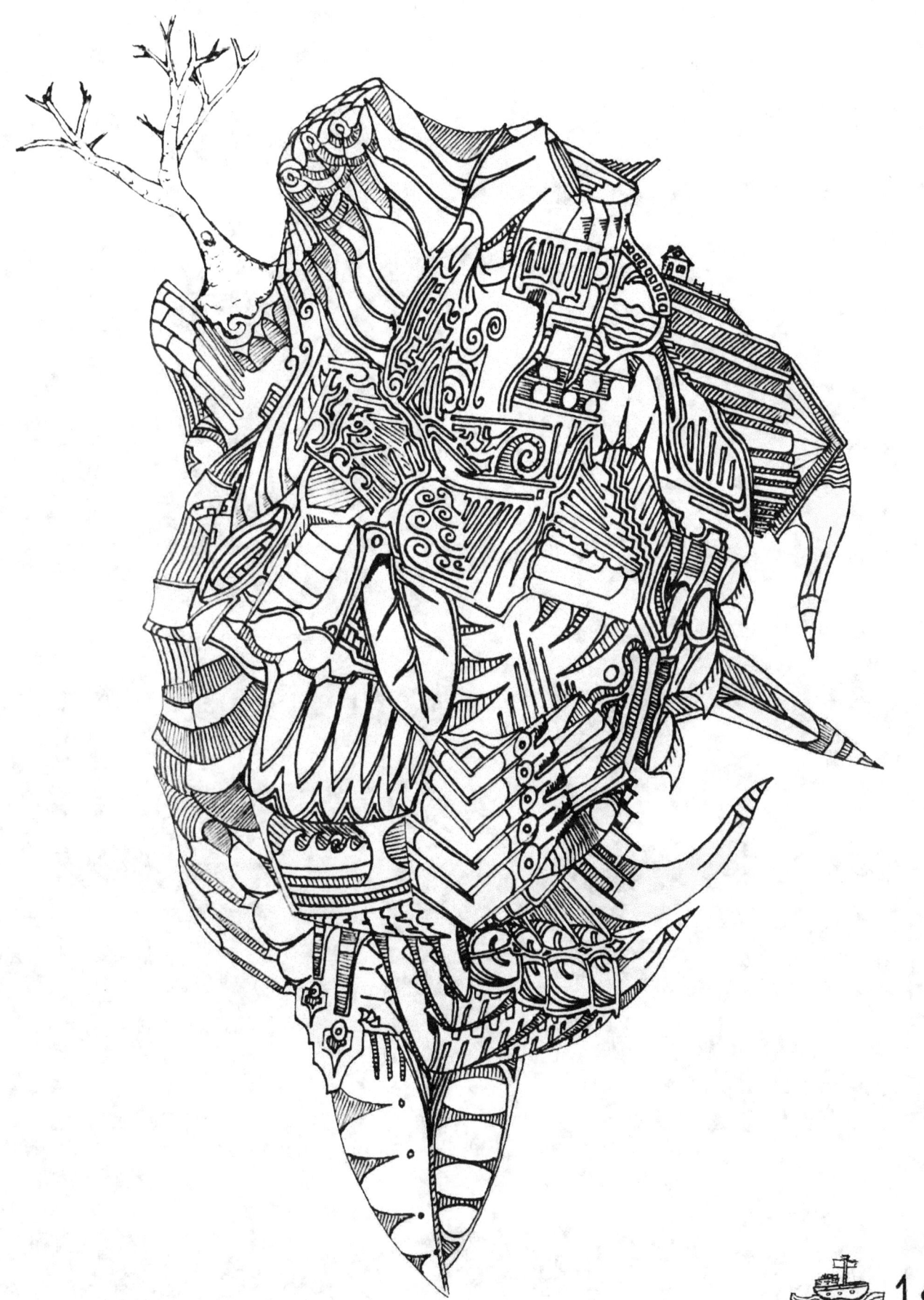

16

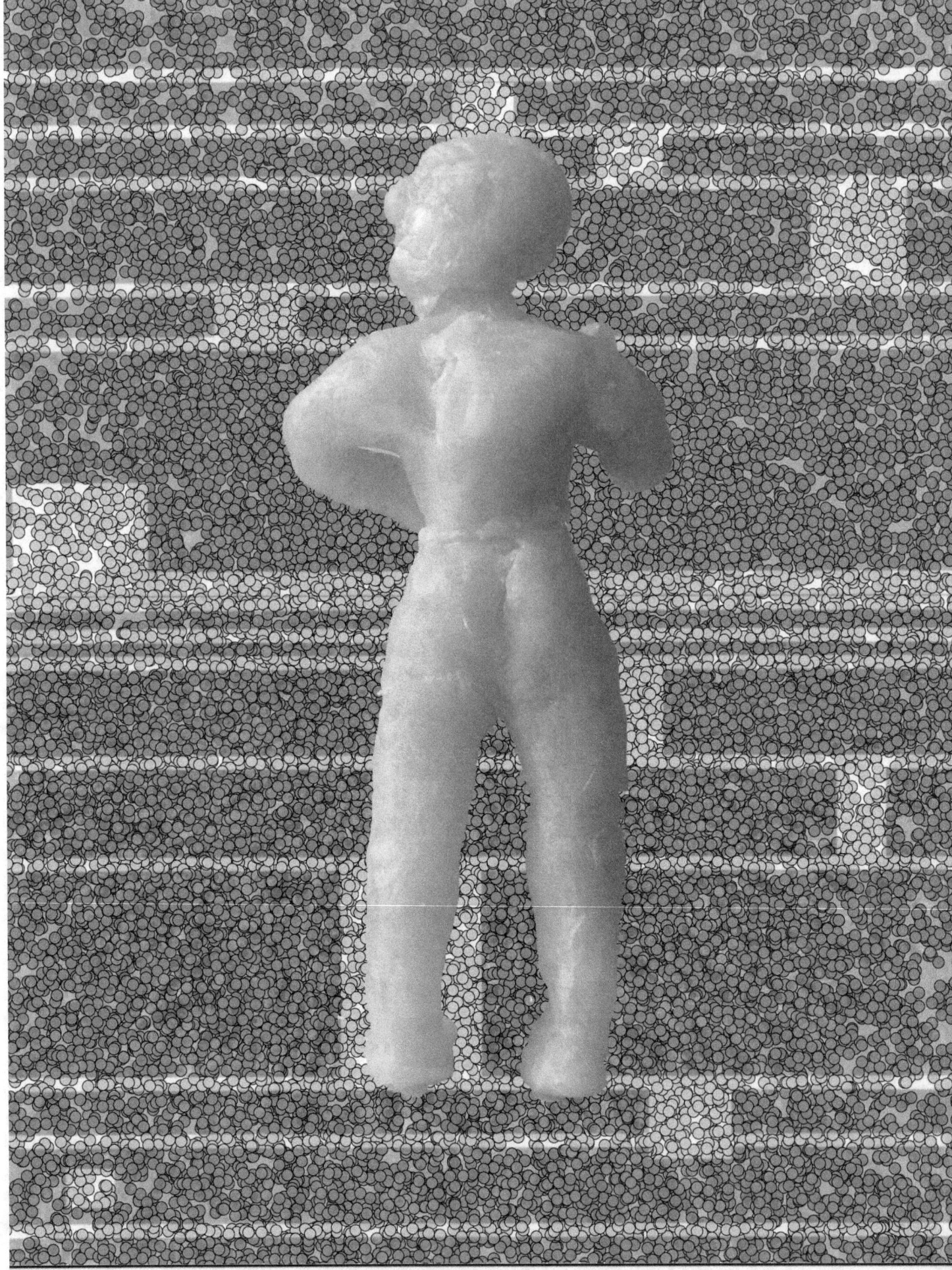

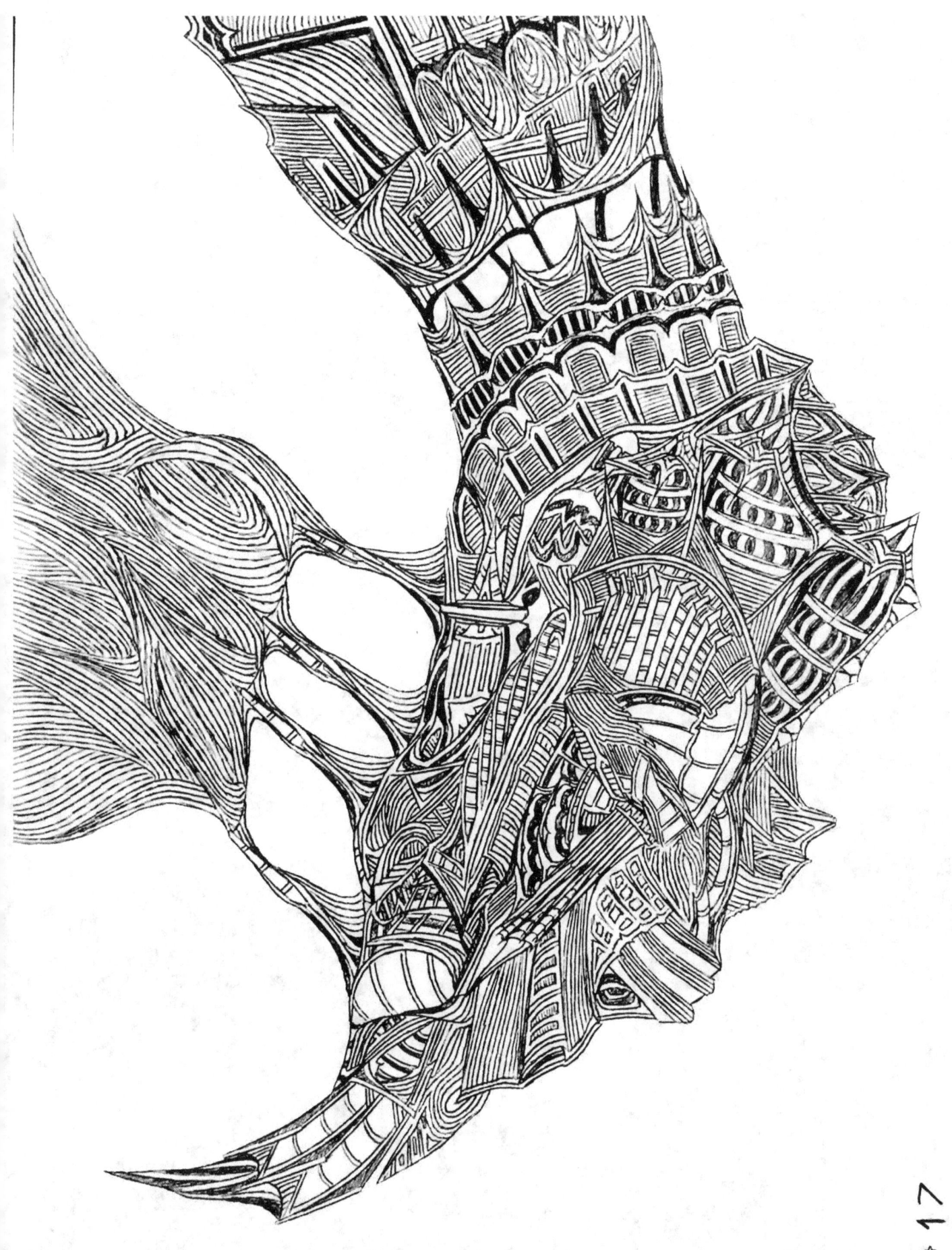

17

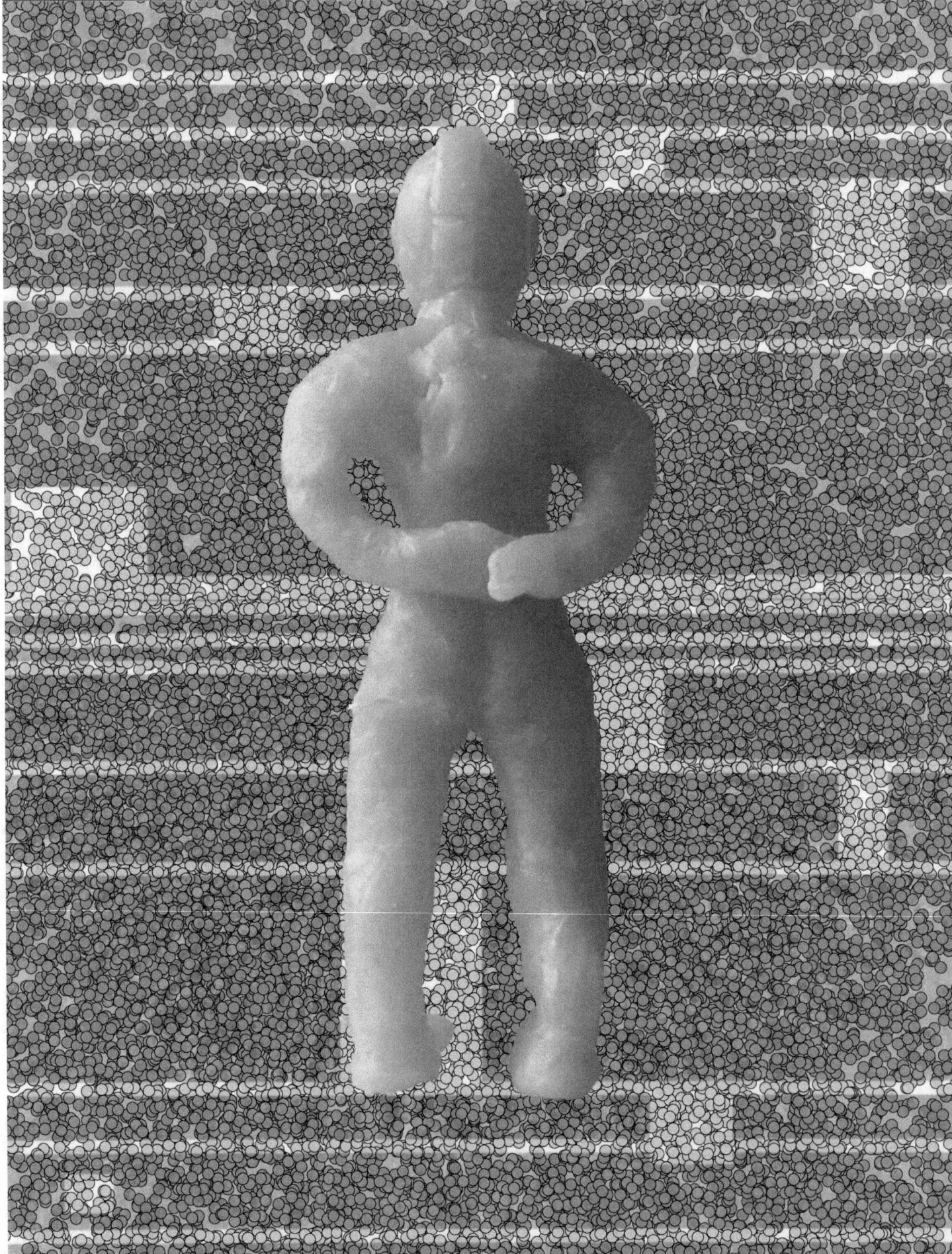

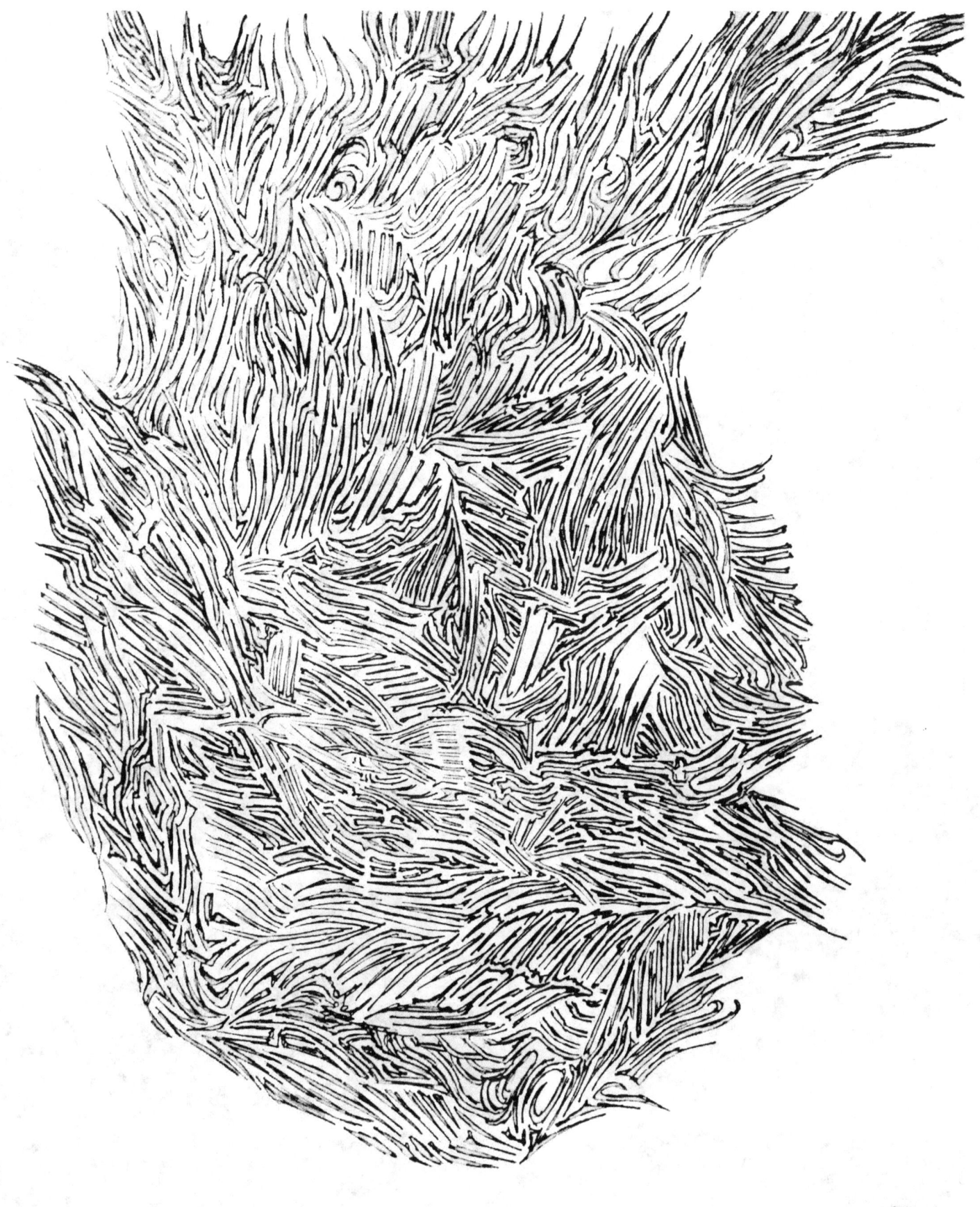

18

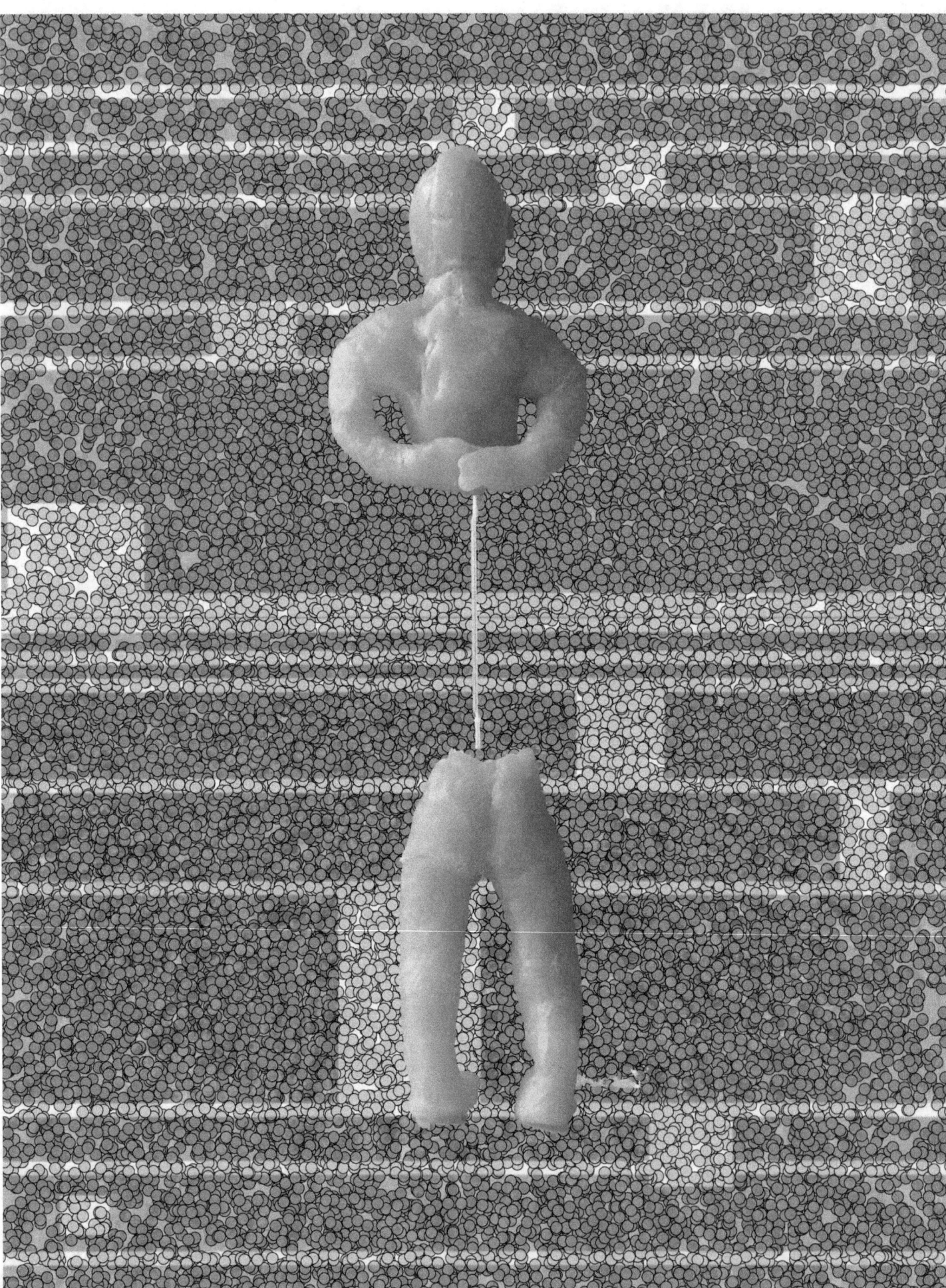

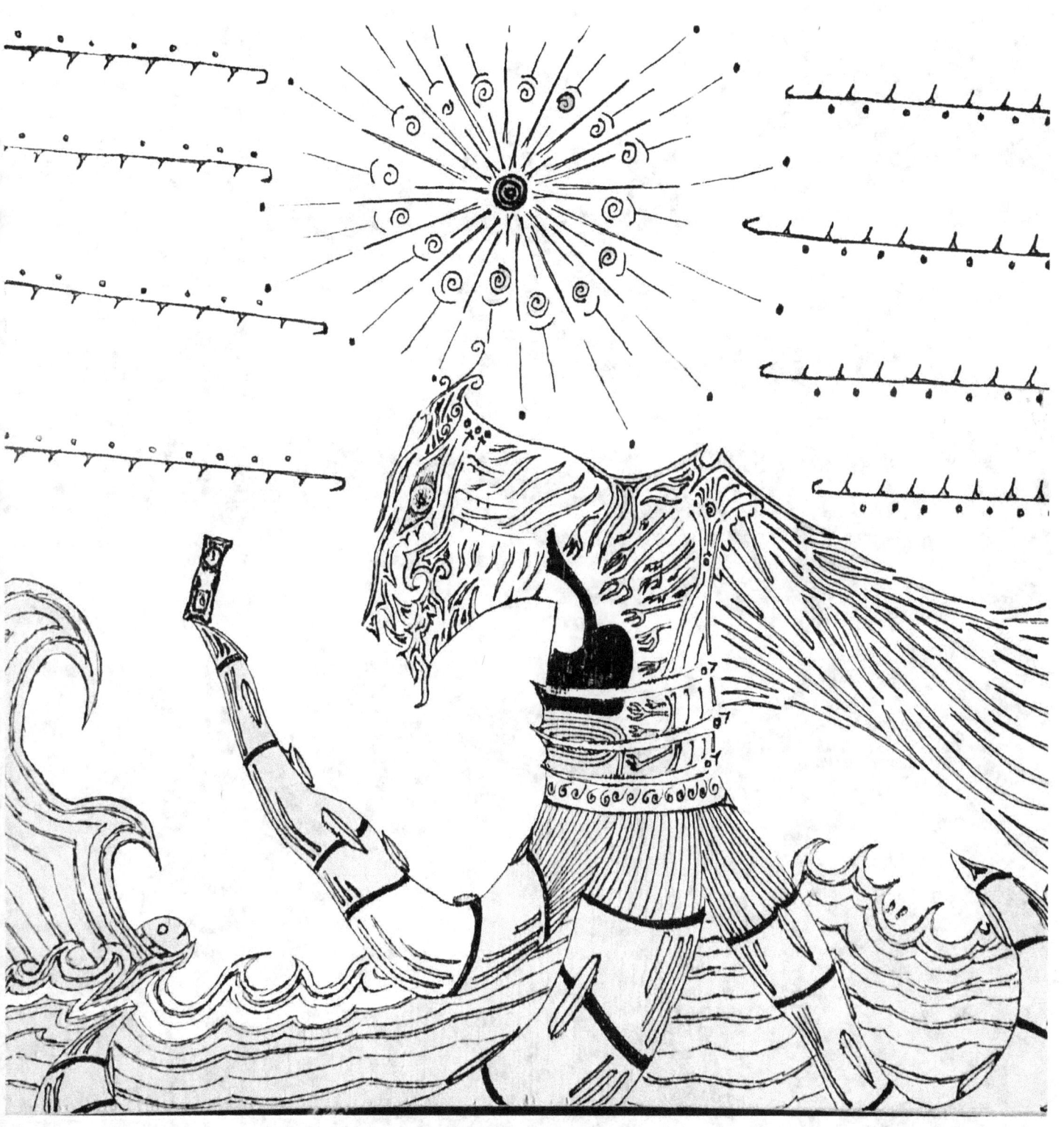

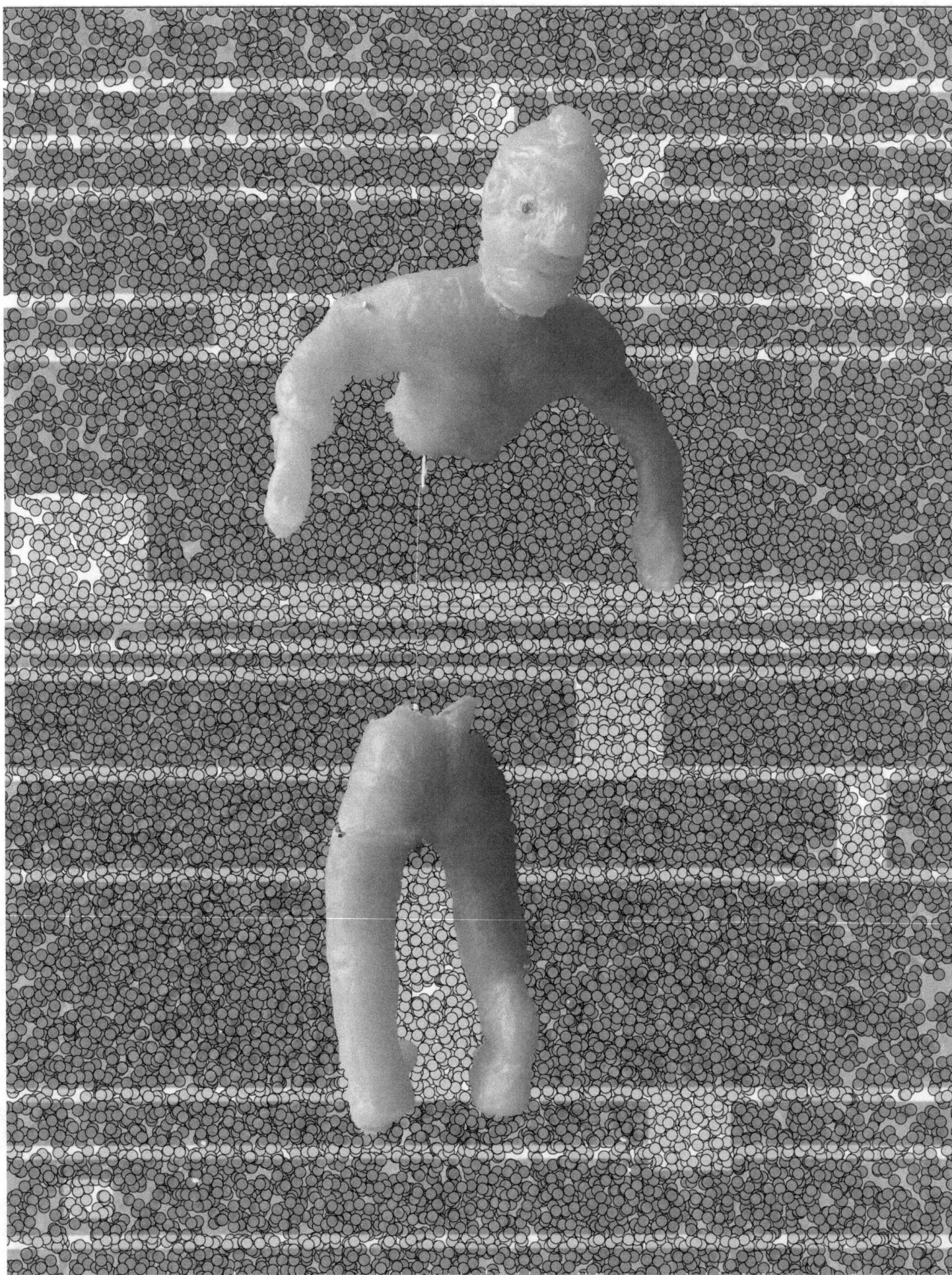

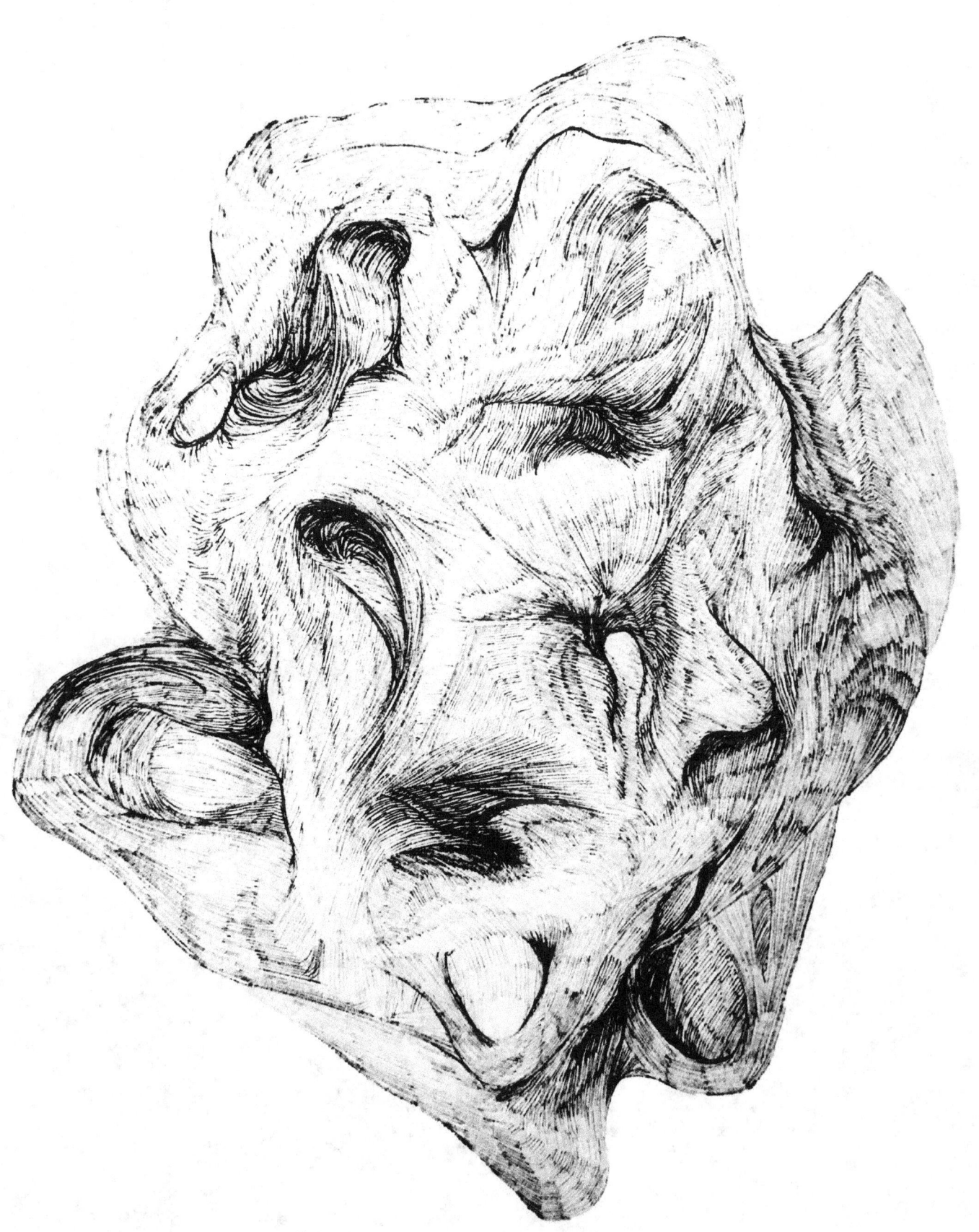

20

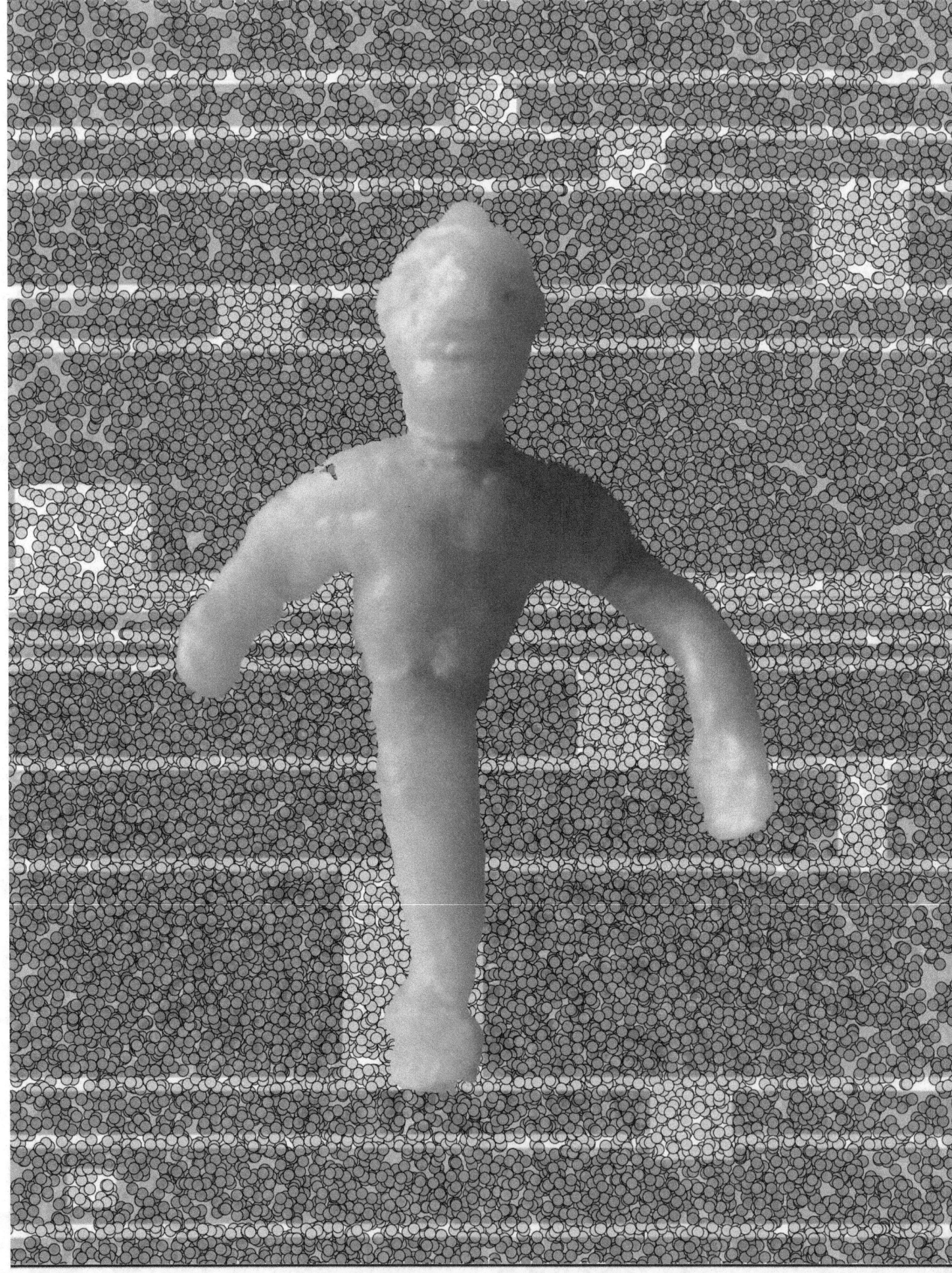

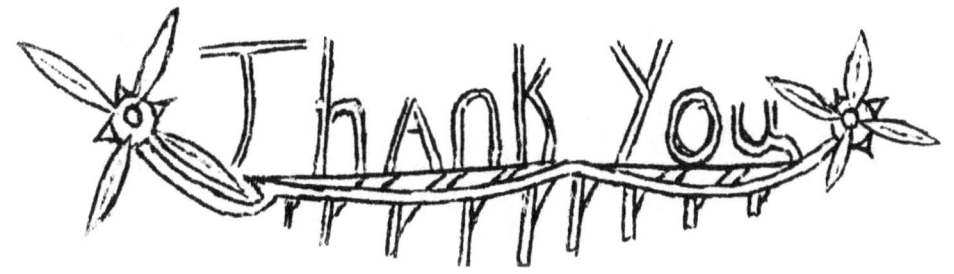

I hope you enjoyed this book!

If you want to see more, or want to know of any future books or work by aux you can find me on these platforms!

- Twitter- Aux_Design
- Instagram- aux_design
- Pinterest- aux_design

I would love to see your results! ^.^

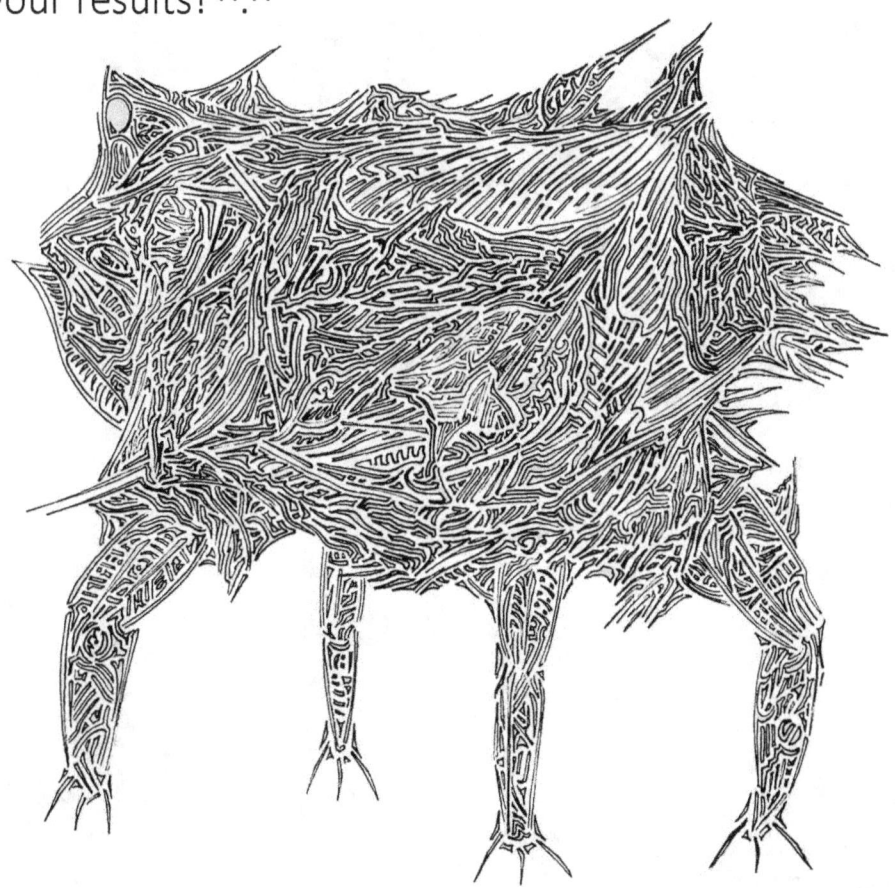